W9-AZO-008

The Amazing Afterlife of Animals

Messages and Signs from our Pets on the Other Side

By Karen A Anderson

Copyright © 2017 by Karen A Anderson
Cover design: James Ryan

All rights reserved. This book or any portion thereof
may not be reproduced or used in any manner whatsoever
without the express written permission of Karen A Anderson and the
publisher except for the use of brief quotations in a book review.

Printed in the United States of America

First Printing, 2017

ISBN-13: 978-1547280780
ISBN-10: 1547280786

Painted Rain Publishing

Awards for

The Amazing Afterlife of Animals

- ❖ Winner 2018 International Book Awards – Animals/Pets
- ❖ Winner 2018 Next Generation Indie Book Awards
- ❖ Winner 2018 New Apple Book Award – New Age
- ❖ Winner 2018 Pinnacle Book Achievement Award
- ❖ Winner 2018 Indie Book Awards
- ❖ Winner 2018 Beverly Hills Book Awards – Grief
- ❖ Silver Medal Winner 2017 Nautilus Book Awards
- ❖ Silver Medal Winner 2018 Readers Favorite Awards
- ❖ Finalist 2018 Beverly Hills Book Awards – Pets
- ❖ Finalist 2018 International Book Awards – New Age
- ❖ Finalist 2018 International Book Awards – Spirituality
- ❖ Finalist 2018 International Book Awards – Best Cover Design
- ❖ Finalist 2018 Best Book Awards Non-Fiction – Pets
- ❖ Finalist 2018 Best Book Awards Non-Fiction – New Age
- ❖ Finalist 2018 Best Book Awards Non-Fiction Best Cover Design

Praise for

The Amazing Afterlife
of Animals

"Karen's new book *The Amazing Afterlife of Animals* is a heartfelt joy to read, as she views the other side of the veil from the animal's perspective. I have known Karen for a long time and can attest to her love of animals and accuracy of the information she receives. Give this book a read. Your heart and your critters will appreciate the insight you will gain.

**~ Ron Sohler, author of *The Reluctant Shaman*
and *Returning to Peig Sayers***

"This book is fantastic! I loved it! I cried and laughed through the entire book. There are many wonderful messages from pets on the Other Side, helping us through our grief. Thank you, Karen!"

~ Denise P.

"The authenticity of Karen's gifts flow through countless touching stories of animals lovingly communicating with their humans from the Beyond. The stories in *The Amazing Afterlife of Animals* can provide healing for those who have lost a beloved animal companion. And for those with living pets, the insights here could transform and enrich the existing bond. Karen's humility and kindness make this an intimate, uplifting portrait of her work as an animal communicator, psychic and medium."

~ Amy Bonaccorso

"When I finished reading Karen Anderson's book 'The Amazing Afterlife of Animals' aloud for myself and my cat, Squeekie Girl, I told her that I would give it 4 Hearts Up, and she said, "I give it 4 Paws Up!"

~ JM

"I could not put this book down. After reading this wonderful book, I am no longer sad about my pets who have passed away. Thank you so much for writing this insightful book. It is truly uplifting to learn that our beloved pets are still with us. This book will help a multitude of people understand what happens to their pets after they pass away.

"Karen's new book, *The Amazing Afterlife of Animals*, will open minds to an entirely new dimension and prove that our pets continue to send us messages. I am strongly recommending this book to all my pet parent friends and family."

~ JoAnn Yasui

"Whenever we lose one of our beloved companion animals, we grieve deeply and nothing can fill the loss or their absence. Karen Anderson's new book The Amazing Afterlife of Animals helps us to know they are not gone but are happy, doing well and still remain lovingly connected to us from the Spirit World, which can help us to heal and open our hearts again."

~ KF

"Karen has a unique talent to be able to share not only her gifts of being able to communicate with animals and humans that have passed, but also the ability to explain the process. Her stories from those she connects with on the Other Side are invaluable and bring great peace to those of us that remain here. Karen is a gem, and we are all blessed by her presence and her gifts."

~ Karen Van Winkle

*"I loved Karen Anderson's latest book, '**The Amazing Afterlife of Animals**.' Her conversational writing style made this an easy, fun and informative read. Karen seamlessly weaves her personal journey into the countless stories of her communication with animals and humans on the other side — a journey that led to the fulfillment of her life's purpose.*

"Karen's stories are at times moving, heartbreaking, exciting, funny, but always honest and real. Not only is Karen a conduit between her client and their beloved on the Other Side, she often plays the role of counselor, helping her client in a caring and compassionate way. Having had many sessions with Karen, I know this first hand. A must-read for anyone who has lost a loved one, pet or person."

~ **Teresa Mena**

"A wonderful, fascinating and enjoyable read from acclaimed Animal Communicator and author Karen Anderson. Karen writes from the heart! This book truly brings to light the bond we have with animals, and I found it to be just what I needed in a time of turmoil and uncertainty — a reminder of the divine order and unconditional love that connects us to our source and to each other. Animals are often the finest examples of pure love, and Karen's connection to them is inspiring and extraordinary. Thank you, Karen, for your wisdom, compassion, and for providing a voice for the animals and a fascinating glimpse into your world."

~ **Dyan W.**

"One of the things I most admire about Karen is her courage to honor her calling and her willingness to share about her journey. This book is rife with real stories that enable us to witness the unseen world of animals. This book is an invitation to open our hearts and learn to walk with animals as partners with unique gifts. The stories are moving and a tremendous source of encouragement for those of us who dare plumb the depths of connection with animals."

~ **Julie Hendrickson**

"Karen Anderson shares her beginning, her middle, her progress and her setbacks all the way to where she is now. Her journey isn't as quick as you'd think. Like many journeys to find your calling, there are rough roads, failures, denial and, finally, acceptance. The help she gives humans, their pets and animals from the other side will make you cry, laugh and feel the gratitude your pets have for you even when they're gone. As they aren't really gone, you just can't see them anymore. This book told me things I never knew and things I never read in the other books about pet psychics over the years. It was a joy to read. Her process is explained in great detail, and I could not put the book down."

~ **Debbie Golden**

*"After reading '**The Amazing Afterlife of Animals**,' I felt a sense of comfort to learn that death is not the end and that my pets stay connected. I was amazed and fascinated by the stories where animals helped to assist on crime scenes."*

~ **Adrienne**

"Karen Anderson's book ***The Amazing Afterlife of Animals*** is a very touching compilation of stories about the bonds of love between ourselves and our beloved pets. Karen proves that even though our loved ones have passed away, our time with them is not over. She teaches us how to recognize the clues that our deceased loved ones leave us to let us know that they are still with us."

~ **Janice Magill**

*"As I read '**The Amazing Afterlife of Animals**,' the feelings of love for my many past companions pulled my present cats to me. They were cuddled with me the entire time. I felt understanding more about their attachments to me brought us even closer together. Karen opened up my heart, and I am so grateful for the knowledge of the forever soul and love of my fur kids. I have so many friends from my past animal shelter employment who will benefit greatly from your knowledge."*

~ **Cindi K.**

"Karen's book *The Amazing Afterlife of Animals* is an imperative read for anyone agonizing over the loss of a departed pet. She reminds us so clearly that it is about the love. The animals focus on the love and the fun, while we get stuck in the 'last days' or making a decision to help them transition. If you have been unsure at all, this is a must-read. I believe it will bring peace to your heart regarding your departed pet."

~ Fran Bell

"I loved this book and could not put it down. It made me laugh and cry with such wonderfully warm stories and comforting messages from our pets."

~ Clydene Lloyd

"The chapter on grief is so helpful. Though I personally am all too familiar with the grief road, it will be helpful to many to understand it better. Also, I like the chapters which included what to say and not to say when a loved one's dear pet dies. Those hold true for human losses also."

~ Barb E.

For my love,
Danny R.

Dedication

This book is dedicated to those who have endured the pain and overwhelming sorrow of saying goodbye to a beloved animal companion.

I also dedicate this book to all the animals on Earth and on the Other Side who have loved us and made our lives so much richer.

Dedication

Acknowledgements

There are many wonderful people I would like to thank for all their love and support as this manuscript came to life. The book most certainly would not be what it is today without all the feedback and insights from all who helped me connect the dots. I'm truly grateful to all of you.

To my mom, Ursula Wassner: I love you with all my heart. You are my best friend, and I am so lucky to have such an incredible mom like you. Words cannot express my deep gratitude for all your love and support over the years and in the writing of this book. Thank you for allowing me to honor my gifts, unusual as they may be. Because of your love, I can live my life to the fullest. I will love you forever.

To my aunt and uncle, Dave and Renate Michaut: Thank you so much for all your help with the manuscript and all the revisions. Renate, your sharp eye caught so many errors I would have surely missed. Thank you for all the feedback and listening to me go on and on about the book. Most of all, thank you for being there when I needed you the most. Your love, support and kindness are so deeply appreciated. If not for you, I would be a very lost soul and would not have the beauty that surrounds me. I love you both so very much.

I also want to thank Annie Kagan for all the kindness, love and support you have so graciously given me. I am eternally grateful.

To Jill Mangino: Thank you for your beautiful light and generous heart. The Universe brought you into my life at exactly the right moment.

To my favorite shaman, Ron Sohler: Our connection is literally out of this world. Thank you for introducing me to the paranormal side of life, for all the laughs, crazy moments, peaches, Archangels, Ireland, Manresa Castle, being zapped, dragons, gnomes, faeries, elves, motorboats and hat stealing. Who would have ever thought that such a skeptic would become such a believer? I can't wait to see what you and I will write a book about. The critters and I love you very much.

To my cold case partner, Angel Nieves: Working with you has been such an honor and a blessing. You are an amazing man, so talented, so very special. I am so grateful to have you in my life. I love you, my friend.

To my very dear friend, Teresa Mena: I am so very grateful for all your love and support over the years and most recently with the writing of this book. Your willingness to help and your patience when I kept sending revisions is so appreciated. You are an incredible woman who has inspired me to new heights. I am so very honored to call you my friend. I love you so much.

To my very dear friend, Diane Sposili: I could not have done this without you. Your feedback was crucial in every chapter. You're amazing, and I am eternally grateful. I love you, Larry, Donald and all the kitties so much.

To my very dear friends and brave souls who reviewed the first draft: Lynn Knoblauch, Leslee Bouttu, Maryann Bouttu, Diana Roberts, Carla Heins and Eric. Thank you so much for imparting your wisdom and feedback. Each one of you has helped me create what is now the final draft, and I am forever grateful. I love you all so much.

A special note to Eric: Thank you for opening your home and your heart to so many deserving and special cats. You are an amazing man.

To Julie Smith: On behalf of so many lost, scared and hungry cats, thank you for being their mom, caretaker and for providing a warm place for them to live out their lives.

To my very dear psychic friends who inspire me with their incredible talent: Barbara Mackey, Seth Michael, Aurora — Sharon Lewis, and Teresa Kleve. I love you all so much.

To all of my beloved clients: Thank you for trusting me to connect with your animal and human loved ones, for without you the stories in this book could not be shared. For all your love and support over the past two decades, thank you.

A special note of love and appreciation to: Laurie Acken, Shell Andrews, Pam & Bob Arthur, Jo Albertson, Angie Bearl, Katie Brambrink, Joan B., Fran Bell, Amy Bonaccorso, Maria Bonino, Judy Casale, Kevin Cook, Connie Crandall, Caroline Davidson, Steven DeRose, Nancy Dorrien, Rayette Eaton, Sandy Fenstermacher, Karen & Jim Frazier, Jodi Gartman, Kristen Gray, Frank Grine, Kathy Fiedler, Steve Filkins, Carrol Haines, Phyllis Hamlin, Debbie & Richard Hassler, Kit Jagoda, Gail & Toby Johnson, Katie Montana Jordan, Ellen Kelley, Tiki Kim, Randy Kovach, Ruth Kraft, Gayle Lammers, Jane Laremore, Mary Lilga, Tristan David Luciotti & Amy Castellano, Eizabeth Mazak, Jacki McManus, Gillian Mosapor, Carla Negrete & Nick Johnson, Joanne Nelson, Jody Newman, Linda & Gary Ocasio, Monica Parfait, Pam Ribbey, Cindy Richards, Rachel Searles, Jyl Straub, Kathy Schatel, Carolyn Smith, Julie Smith, Phyllis Stuart, Adrienne S., Nicole Strickland, Karissa Thomas, Nancy Tramontano, Nancy Tuccillo, Denise Webber, Sarah Welte, Michael White, Ruth Wilfong, Jay Verburg, Edgar Yohe, and Patty B. Zlamany.

A special thank you to Ronnie Rennae for your huge contribution to this manuscript. I'm forever grateful to you for all your help.

A special thank you to Dannion and Kathryn Brinkley for the wonderful endorsement and ongoing support.

A special thank you and photo credits to Richard Hassler for the hat-stealing photo on the back cover.

A special thank you to Cheryl Knight for proofreading and editing.

I want to thank James Ryan for the beautiful cover design and Noel Morado for the layout and design.

To anyone I forgot to mention, forgive me. It was not intentional. Send me a note, and I'll add your name to the next edition.

Finally, I would like to thank our God and Divine Creator, my Spirit Guides, the Archangels and all the souls on the Other Side who helped me realize my purpose in this lifetime.

Table of Contents

Foreword
by Dr. Annie Kagan

Author of the international bestselling book,
"The Afterlife of Billy Fingers:
How My Bad-Boy Brother Proved to Me
There's Life After Death"

I've always loved animals: cats, dogs, elephants, horses, tigers and, okay, not really snakes. So several years ago I went to a talk given by an animal communicator. I didn't really know what that was, but it sounded good. She had all kinds of photos of animals responding to her: elephants bowing, touching her head with theirs, horses kissing her face, a harbor seal lying in her lap on a beach in California. Very impressive.

So when my cat, Johnny Angel, was having problems, I searched for an animal communicator.

A mutual friend suggested that I contact Karen Anderson. When I called Karen to make an appointment, she asked if I was the Annie Kagan who was the author of *The Afterlife of Billy Fingers: How My Bad Boy Brother Proved to Me There's Life After Death.*

When I confirmed that I was, Karen excitedly told me that my book was one of her favorites. She also believes our loved ones exist on the Other Side, sending us signs, letting us know they are around and continuing their journey until we meet again. Karen loved the story, especially how I doubted that my dead brother Billy was real and not imagined; how Billy kept sending me signs and messages that were so precise, so remarkable, they provided concrete proof of his existence. Even when I tried not to believe it, Billy left me with no doubt that the tour of the afterlife he was taking me on was real. We indeed are all divine eternal beings.

Karen also confided that she had the ability to speak with animals that had gone over to the Other Side. This didn't seem out of the realm of possibilities to me, since I believe our pets are souls and we meet them in the afterlife.

My session with Karen was awesome in so many unpredictable ways. She gave me messages directly from Johnny Angel, as if he was talking to me, telling me things that no one but he and I would understand. Within a few minutes I was crying. Karen couldn't fully grasp the significance of the messages she communicated, but I certainly did. Through Karen, I understood that Johnny was feeling less important than my other two cats, who were both adopted before him. Once I was aware of what he was feeling, he and I solved the problem quickly.

After my session, Karen asked if I would read her book, *The Amazing Afterlife of Animals*. Because she helped my kitty so much, I agreed. At that point I didn't know I was in for quite a treat. From the touching account of her childhood experience with a dove, to her fascinating path to becoming an animal psychic, to her invaluable wisdom about our beloved pets, amazing marvelousness jumps from the pages of her inspiring book.

Karen will take your relationship with your pets, on this side and the next, to new horizons!

Foreword
by Patricia Carrington, Ph.D.

Adjunct Professor, Department of Psychiatry
Robert Wood Johnson Medical School
Rutgers University, Piscataway, NJ
Author of "The Secret Inner Life of Pets"

There is an electricity in the air these days, and I think it reflects a difference that is occurring in this era — a greater openness, it would seem, to the unseen forces that influence us.

I know a lot about this particular development, because for years I was involved in the greatly limiting "if you don't see it, it doesn't exist" school of thought, which scientists, including psychologists like myself, used to spend so much of their time on.

Increasingly, this is not the case today. I myself, for example, am not the cautious "realistic" person that I was in the days when I taught at Princeton University and pretended to be just a "hard scientist" when there was much more to me than that. Much of this change has had to do with the passing of my very dear pet cat, Dandy, who left this earth on Good Friday of 2015.

Dandy seems to symbolize many other pets who exhibit some special knowledge, and in my case, he was actually the reason I came to know Karen Anderson and the world of animal communication and why I wrote a book on the subject of the profound inner life of our pets.

I am, by profession, both a clinical psychologist and an author, and one might call me an innovator as well, always interested in what is in the forefront of things — new ways, new frontiers. But what is fascinating to me is the way my perspective has expanded in the past few years. Is there something new in the air?

I think there is and that this "something" is being ushered in by unsung heroes, and in many cases, it seems to reflect the wisdom of our own pets. At times I truly believe that these animals have far more profound a role to play in our lives than we have suspected.

Are they perhaps Guardians of us in one sense? Have they perhaps come to us from another realm to open our hearts in a unique way? These are very real possibilities.

As a psychologist, I have always been especially interested in the meaning behind the incredible bond between domesticated animals and their humans. It is one of the oldest bonds that exist as far as we know. Although it may be hard for the human race to admit it, our companion animals play a role that is so special in our lives that often when they pass away their loss is quite often as unbearable as the pain which we feel when we lose our most beloved humans.

Why Should This Be?

One of the reasons I believe is the collection of experiences stored in our genes — a memory of the soul, as it were. This may have been from a time when we were as simple and honest and genuine as one of our pets are. In many ways, although we don't often admit it openly, our pets represent a "better" us, a more real, more simple, more clean and clear version of ourselves, and we deeply respect that part of us and long for it. We respect the integrity these pets have, their simple, loving nature, although we can't seem to admire the average human being that much, nor do we trust them as easily as we do animals. There is a purity in the soul of the animal that few people show in such an authentic manner.

The simple fact is that all things being equal, we trust an animal's love above that of most humans. We know their integrity and do not doubt it.

Actually, they are amazing role models. What person do you know who is as forgiving as a pet can be? What person is as unquestioning in their loyalty? How many people give us complete daily relief from the hypocrisy so prevalent in our lives yet so strikingly absent in the animal world?

Karen Anderson's newest book, **The Amazing Afterlife of Animals**, contains fascinating information from another realm. It gives us a whole new perspective on life after life, and therefore, of course, on life down here right during life. I would urge you to enjoy the engaging adventures reported within this book. Along the way, and very importantly, they will be eye-opening for you.

Introduction:
Welcome to My World

Did a deceased dog just tell me what his mom had for breakfast? Can a dog that has recently passed away tell me his mom has a potentially life-threatening disease? Can a deceased cat provide enough evidence to solve a murder?

Wow! That stuff sounds crazy. In fact, if it had not happened to me, I would probably question the sanity of the author. But since it did indeed happen to me, I guess I have some explaining to do. I'll share those stories and more as we travel back and forth between the physical world where we live and the Other Side where our departed animals reside.

Welcome to my world — a complex and multidimensional realm of animals, their energy, death, dying and, of course, the afterlife. I'll be sharing a little bit of everything with you on this journey. Keep in mind that I am no more an expert on any of this than the next psychic may be, but I do have actual proof to back up these experiences. Granted, it's not the scientific evidence skeptics are looking for, nor is it something that grew in a petri dish. It won't satisfy the cynics, but it is my evidence that I experienced firsthand with thousands of clients over that past two decades.

Why Do We Want to Communicate With Departed Pets?

Even in death, you are the most important person in the world to your pets. I can't think of a single reason that I wouldn't want to communicate with them after they die. The reasons we want to connect are as unique as we are, but there are a few main goals that most of us have in common.

Primarily, we want to know that our pets are safe, pain-free or with our loved ones on the Other Side. We want them to know how much we love them and miss them. We want to feel good about the life we provided for them, especially if things did not end as peacefully as we would have hoped. Our pets provided us with so much love, companionship and treasured moments that we want to express our gratitude and deepen our connection. Our pets were with us through the good times and bad, always happy to see us and longing for our attention. Our bond is so strong, we feel a sense of responsibility to ensure their wellbeing even after they die. It makes us feel closer to them, it honors them, and it celebrates the time we shared here on Earth.

There Is No Coincidence That You Are Reading This Today

Our departed animals guide us to those we can learn from the most. I believe that if you are reading this right now, there is a spiritual awakening occurring within you — a hunger for answers and a thirst for knowledge about what our pets experience in the afterlife. This quest becomes like an insatiable appetite, and each new piece of information leads you further down the path.

At least that's how it was for me. The more I learned, the more I wanted to know. Chances are your loved ones on the Other Side guided you to pursue this path and even to read this book, as they know that I can help you understand more about what happens when your pets die and leave their physical bodies. Your departed pets and human loved ones also know that I can deliver their messages to you and reassure you that their energy continues after their physical death.

Since I began my journey two decades ago, communication with the soul or spirit of an animal has become more and more accepted in our society. Maybe it's because many of us are hoping that our animals are still with us and around us after they die. Perhaps it's because so many of us are experiencing afterlife communication with our departed pets.

My advice is to absorb as much information as you can from me or any other reliable source. Focus on that which resonates within you, pursue the areas that catch your interest, and leave the rest behind. For each of us, the journey is a little bit different. No one has all the answers, and you should run as fast as you can away from anyone who says they do.

Let the Animals Be Our Guides on the Other Side

As you read through the chapters, it is my hope to open your mind so you can perhaps view the idea of animals existing in the afterlife, as it actually happens. Maybe you already believe that an afterlife somehow continues in a heavenly place. If so, then you'll find the stories in this book will validate many of your perceptions of eternity. If you don't believe or are not quite sure, I hope to gently nudge you, and in some cases, I may even push you past your comfort level of what happens when our pets die.

I've selected some of the most memorable and inspiring moments from actual sessions and my personal experiences over the past two decades to share with you. I hope to take some of the mystery, fear and sorrow away when your devoted animal companion passes away and leaves our physical realm.

I've also included a behind-the-scenes peek into my background growing up, my law enforcement days and, ultimately, how I was guided to follow this unique path into the psychic realm. Perhaps you will identify with similar experiences in your life, which may allow you to identify your purpose in life with greater clarity.

In most cases, names were changed for privacy, but the actual accounts and messages remain pure and untouched. While you may be tempted to skip ahead to view a section you are curious about, I recommend that you read the stories in the order presented. The chapters build upon each other, and the experiences are strategically placed. If you bounce between chapters, you may miss crucial information. Following along in the order written will ensure you get the most comprehensive insight as to what your pets experience on the Other Side. I share these anecdotes in general terms, so keep in mind that no two pets are alike and every situation is unique.

Ultimately, my greatest hope is that if you are in the depths of despair over the loss of your precious animal companion, these stories will illuminate a space to invoke healing within your heart. You deserve to live a happy and joyful life knowing that your departed pets remain connected to you.

In the last section of the book, I'll provide tools to help you navigate through your pain and loosen the grip of grief. I think many of us would agree we would do it all over again in spite of all the pain we endure after the loss of a pet.

When I look back on the unique path that I have taken, it is evident that none of these amazing experiences would have happened if I had not pursued my talents. One simple decision catapulted me into a lifetime of love, healing and joy. I said "**yes**" to my gifts.

The Gift

We are all born with a gift. We come into this world with a divine gift from God, our Creator, deep within our soul. I believe our primary purpose in life is to honor our gift and to utilize our talents to their fullest potential.

Our divine gift may be any number of talents, such as painting, writing, music or teaching. It is our unique calling card and is bestowed upon us to enrich our lives and those around us.

Sometimes we travel down the road of life unaware of the gifts that lie just beneath the surface of our soul. We feel lost in the vastness of the world and find ourselves searching everywhere but within our own hearts for a sense of belonging and self-worth.

When we embrace our gift, a synchronous cycle begins, and where we were once lost, we now find joys and spiritual blessings that somehow escaped us before. Our life force radiates into the Universe like an enormous web of love and opens a whole new consciousness before us. Over time, all of that love returns to us tenfold and completes the cycle.

It doesn't matter what your gift is; what matters is that you identify and honor your talent to the fullest degree. By honoring your gift, you celebrate your true self. To disregard your gift is to dismiss the most rewarding and gratifying opportunity bestowed upon you in this lifetime.

Discovering your gift is easy. What do you love? What brings you joy? What makes your heart sing? Your gift is the one thing that you can do with minimal effort, yet it produces maximum results.

Are you a natural born chef, talented singer or an amazing tennis player? Do you find joy in working with technology, graphic arts or science?

Once you identify your gift, pursue your talent passionately. Don't let anyone stand in the way of you and your gift. It won't always be easy; in fact, there will be many bumps in the road ahead. You will most certainly encounter many obstacles and dead-ends, but trust in yourself, persevere, and new avenues will appear.

On your road of life, there will likely be naysayers or skeptics lurking around every curve. Just remember that those negative souls are usually ignoring their own gifts and have fallen off their spiritual path. Stay true to yourself and focused on your final destination.

I strongly believe in the power of vision boards and manifesting the future. If you can visualize it, then it can happen.

As you read through the stories in this book, I will share some of the struggles and mistakes I made along the way. I view those struggles as opportunities not obstacles, and because of them, I continued ahead even stronger than before.

When you arrive at the final chapter, I hope that you will be able to clearly identify what your divine gift is. It's never too late to start honoring your gift. I followed my spiritual calling, and you can too.

~ Karen Anderson

Part I

Part 1

Chapter 1:
Nowhere Else
They Would Rather Be

Mourning is love
with no place to go.
~ Author Unknown

It was getting late, and Bandit nestled into his favorite spot on the corner of the bed. With sleepy eyes, the large cat watched his human mom turn down the sheets and adjust her pillows. The warm night air carried the scent of lavender and fresh grass as it drifted across the room. This was his favorite time of day, when everything was calm and the moon was rising in the Eastern sky. Summertime on the farm was spectacular, and everything was in full bloom.

Lying contently beside him was his best friend, Choo Choo. She was a black cat with splashes of orange and white, often referred to as a tortie or tortoiseshell cat. She had almond-shaped eyes and a small compact body.

Just as Bandit was ready to drift off to sleep, he heard his human mom begin to cry. He turned around to see tears rolling down her face. She held a photo of the two cats in her hands. It had been only three short months since Bandit died, and Choo Choo had passed away just a couple months before him.

"I miss you both so much," she said softly. "I just wish you were here with me." The loss of both of her beloved cats was almost too much to bear.

Every night their mom would pick up the framed photo and talk to them about her day. What she didn't realize was that they already knew what she had been doing — for Bandit and Choo Choo were never far away. Eventually, the tears would come as she longed for just one more moment with the two of them.

"Oh no; mom's crying again tonight," Bandit said to Choo Choo.

Choo Choo slowly opened her golden-colored eyes and glanced over to their mom.

"Bandit, she doesn't know we are here," Choo Choo said. "She thinks we are in some faraway place or gone forever. Let's try to let her know we are right here."

Both cats got up and went over to console their human mom.

"Mom, we are right here," Choo Choo said, as she rubbed up against her mom's hand. "We are always with you."

"There is nowhere else we would rather be," Bandit said, as he gently pressed his huge head against her tear-stained face.

Over the next few weeks, the two cats tried everything they could think of to communicate with their mom. They tried brushing up against her, tickling her face with their whiskers, knocking pens off the desk, and appearing in spirit form so that she could see them out of the corner of her eyes.

As time went by, their mom began to sense that her beloved cats were trying to communicate with her from the Other Side. She sat down at the computer one evening and searched *communicating with deceased pets*.

Her search found many hundreds of listings for Animal Communicators. She clicked on several websites until she came to one in particular.

When she saw Karen Anderson's picture, she just knew Karen was the Animal Communicator she needed to contact.

Finally, the day of the appointment arrived. Their mom nervously checked the clock every five minutes as she paced around the room.

She dialed the number, and as soon as she heard Karen's warm voice, their mom began to relax. Karen suggested that she take a few deep breaths and sit back and enjoy the session.

"I'm a bit nervous," their mom said. "I've never done anything like this before."

"No worries. I understand completely," Karen replied. "It is normal to be a bit nervous before a session."

The cats listened in as Karen began the session with a prayer and a blessing.

"Who would you like to start with today?" Karen asked.

"Oh, I'm not sure. I love them both so much. Let's start with Choo Choo."

"Wow! Choo Choo is so smart," Karen said. "She is showing me her whiskers and keeps brushing them against my face, and it tickles. Choo Choo says this is how she wakes you up. Do you understand this message?"

"Oh my gosh! Do I understand it? Yes, I do! Choo Choo would wake me up every morning with her whiskers. I miss her so much. Does she know how much I love her?" their mom asked, choking back the tears.

"Yes, she does. She says you talk to her all the time and that she still wakes you up with her whiskers," Karen said.

"I thought I was going crazy, but I can still feel her whiskers brush against my face. Is that really her?" their mom asked barely able to talk.

"Yes, that's her. She says she helps you wake up on time," Karen said.

"Unbelievable. I just can't wrap my head around how this is possible."

"I know it's pretty amazing, even for me," Karen said. "I'm honored to be a part of your journey. Now Choo Choo is showing me a plate of sushi. Does that make any sense to you?" Karen asked.

"Yes! Sushi was her name when I adopted her from the shelter. The name didn't suit her, so I changed it to Choo Choo. Nobody knows that, Karen. How did you know?"

"Choo Choo told me," Karen said. "She says she likes the name Choo Choo much better. She says she is always with you and has tried very hard to get your attention. She wants you to know she can hear you talk about your day."

As the messages continued to roll in, their mom felt a new sense of wonder wash over her.

Next, it was Bandit's turn.

"Bandit is such a gentleman. He says you saved him, and without you, he would have died at a young age."

"Yes, that's true. He showed up as a starving stray cat many years ago," their mom said.

"He is showing me a pen for some reason. Are you a writer? I'm not sure what the pen means," Karen said.

"The pen game!" their mom squealed. "Bandit would knock my pens off my desk all the time. I can't believe this!"

"He has been knocking pens off the table to let you know he is around."

"Yes, he has! I thought it was my imagination. I didn't think they could communicate by moving things. I miss them so much it hurts my heart. I have felt so empty since they died. I've been so lonely."

"Well, now you know your sweet cats are alive and well in spirit," Karen said with a smile. "They both send you so much love; it's washing over me in waves. You're one lucky lady to have such amazing pets that watch over you."

"I'm speechless, Karen," their mom said. "I don't know how to thank you for this experience. I thought they were gone forever, and now you have changed all of that for me."

"It's truly my pleasure," Karen said. "But before you go, can I ask you how you found me?"

"I searched on the Internet, and your website was the one I was drawn to. I really can't explain it. I just knew when I saw your picture that you were the right one."

As the session ended, Karen thanked the cats for sharing their messages. She explained to their mom how she could visualize filling up her cats' hearts with loving thoughts, which was like spiritual fuel.

"Just think about how you top off your tank at the gas station," Karen explained. "Their hearts are the gas tank, and they need your love, or spiritual fuel, to continue their journey on the Other Side."

Their mom nodded her head as she now understood how to send love to her departed cats. Karen also told their mom that she needs to pay attention to all the little messages they send and to thank them for being so thoughtful.

"Honor your grief, as those feelings are part of the healing process. If you are feeling sad, try to end on a happy thought," Karen said. "Think about the joyful memories, celebrate their life, and try not to dwell on the sad moments. Make their life more important than their death."

While she still missed her cats, their mom had a renewed sense of life and a completely different viewpoint about death.

Bandit and Choo Choo watched their mom smile for the first time in a very long time, and they joyfully zipped around her in a blast of cosmic sunshine.

Their mom finally realized that when a pet dies, it is not the end, but a beginning of their new existence as an energetic being. She was no longer pained by the grief of her losses and understood that she will always be connected with her beloved pets. They were always near her, as there is nowhere else they would rather be.

Chapter 2:
A Unique Path to Follow

Some people talk to animals.
Not many listen though.
That's the problem.
~ A.A. Milne, "Winnie the Pooh"

I didn't set out to go down this psychic road, but evidently, it is my calling. When I was very young, I wanted to be a veterinarian. That didn't last long when I discovered I would have to perform surgery. But I always knew that someday I'd be working with animals. I just never thought it would be as a pet psychic.

There were two prominent influences when I was young, the first being Walt Disney and the second my childhood dog. I grew up in the small town of San Dimas about an hour east of Los Angeles, California. We had a black and white collie, named Prince, whom I credit with teaching me how to communicate with animals.

We would have silly conversations, and I assumed everyone could understand his messages. I had many other animals too, including rabbits, cats and tropical fish. I talked to all of my animals back then and never gave it a second thought.

Early Influences

I grew up watching the movie *Dr. Doolittle*, as well as all famous Disney films back in the 1960s like *Jungle Book* and *Bambi*. If you recall, most the animals in those movies could talk, so it never occurred to me that my animals would be any different.

My favorite television shows were *Mr. Ed* the talking horse, *Flipper*, *Gentle Ben* and my all-time favorite *Lassie*. I was fascinated by how these animals would communicate with their humans.

My Childhood Dog

When I was about five years old, my close connection with my childhood dog, Prince, brought about an incident I will never forget. He slept in my room at night, and on one particular occasion, he became restless and began to pace back and forth. I walked nervously across the room and said he needed to lie down on the cool floor by the front door.

I was so worried that he would die that night. I could feel his pain, and it upset my stomach too. He was my best friend, and I could not imagine my life without him. I laid down on the floor next to him and tried to soothe him. I must have fallen asleep, as my next memory was hearing my mom's voice the next morning. I told her that Prince's tummy hurt and that he said he didn't feel right. I told her about how badly my stomach hurt too.

My mom didn't know what to make of all that at the time and said that animals couldn't talk and I shouldn't make up stories. I remember feeling so angry and upset that she didn't believe me. I thought Prince might die if we didn't do something.

Once my mom realized that Prince was in pain, she quickly whisked him off to the veterinarian's office. Fortunately, it was just a bad case of pancreatitis and Prince fully recovered. It would be the first of many experiences when no one believed that I could talk to the animals.

Karen and Prince on the morning after he sent the urgent message.

It was soon after that incident that I began to hide all of my animal communication from everyone. Only my best friend, Laurie, believed that I could talk to the animals. She couldn't hear them the way I could, but at least she believed me.

Why couldn't anyone else hear them talk? What was wrong with me? I must have a disease or some kind of sickness, I thought.

Animals Provided Love and Companionship

I spent all my time with my pets, secretly talking to them and sharing silly stories with each other. I thought our conversations would last forever. But years later I would shut down my abilities for good. Or so I thought.

In my first book, *Hear All Creatures!,* I shared the story about the orange and white tabby cat that I thought I killed when I was about eight years old. I called to the stray cat from across the road, inviting him to play with me. When the cat ran out into the street, a car came out of nowhere and killed him right before my eyes. I was traumatized by the death of that cat and carried that guilt for many years. I swore I would never again attempt to communicate with another animal after that horrible accident.

The Wrong Profession

Many years later and long before I became involved in any psychic work, I held a few jobs in Orange County, California. I worked for different mortgage companies and learned the finance business. Those jobs demanded detailed attention with numbers and are considered left-brained work. The left side of the brain is said to house all of our analytical processing, such as numbers, logic, reasoning and critical thinking abilities, whereas the right side of the brain focuses on the visual, creative, abstract and intuitive processes.

Needless to say, I was never very happy with those jobs. It wasn't very satisfying work, and I often felt empty inside, like something was missing. I'm not a math person, and I don't like working numbers. I like animals. What in the heck was I doing?

Signs Are Always There

Eventually, every company I worked for went out of business. I was either laid off or fired. Oh yes, my mouth has gotten me into a lot of trouble over the years. Sometimes I don't have a filter, and words just fly out. I'm a very straightforward person, and that landed me in the unemployment line once before.

I kept running into one obstacle after another, nothing but dead ends. Now that I look back on it, I can clearly see that my Spirit Guides were trying desperately to get a message through to me: *You're in the wrong profession, Karen.*

At that time, I was completely unaware that I even had Spirit Guides. I probably would have belly laughed if someone told me I had invisible helpers trying to get my attention. I was in a state of oblivion back in those days. Since then, I have come to know my Spirit Guides and work in close collaboration with them for my psychic work.

We all have these spirit helpers or Spirit Guides, whether you are aware of their presence or not. They are that little voice of reason in your head that nudges you along throughout your life. Your Spirit Guides help you find a front-row parking space or that twenty-dollar bill in your pocket. They are responsible for sending you on a different route to work, only to find out later there was a serious accident right where you would have been. These invisible helpers, much akin to angels, are with you to make your life a little easier.

I continued to work in the mortgage industry and collected some mighty big paychecks. I even found myself trying to climb the corporate ladder. It was a time of material wealth, large bonuses and keeping up with the Joneses. When the economy started to crumble in the early 1990s, my once-prosperous career began to fizzle right before my eyes.

A Spiritual Awakening

It was a tough time financially, and I realized I would have to find a more affordable place to live. After much thought, I decided to leave California to move to Colorado. I packed up and headed to Denver where I had another mortgage job lined up.

It was during this time that I began to notice some strange precognitive events happening, although I didn't realize it at the time. I was out shopping one day and came home with a bag full of black kitchen accessories. I purchased several black throw rugs, black towels and black potholders. The strange part was that my kitchen was blue and white. Nothing was black. I had no idea why I did that. I put the items in the closet and forgot about them.

Within a year, I moved from the Denver Metro area into a mountain home in Bailey. It was not something I planned on; the move came about rather unexpectedly. It was a complete shock when I was unpacking at the new house and found the bag of kitchen items I purchased the year before. All the appliances at the new house were black. The accessories, rugs and towels matched perfectly. *Hmm, that's weird*, I thought to myself.

Strange little things like that kept happening over the next few years, but I did not know it was just the beginning of a spiritual awakening. I was being pulled onto my intuitive path with my eyes shut tight. I had no idea that my intuition would kick in soon and in a big way.

Pay Attention to Your Intuition

Eventually, I opened a small mortgage company with a business partner, named Roy. We were doing quite well for a new company, but I kept having an unsettling feeling about work. I couldn't put my finger on it, but I had a sense that something was very wrong. I worked long hours and poured all of my energy into making that company successful. Still, I had this nagging feeling in the back of my mind that wouldn't go away. One day I sat down at the computer to see what Roy was doing with the bank accounts.

It didn't take long before I found several entries in our bank accounts that did not add up. I stared at the screen in disbelief. *Could this be right? No, it can't be,* I thought to myself. *Roy wouldn't do this*. I went through the canceled checks and found out that my business partner was embezzling from the company and me. *How could he do this to me?*

Page by page, I uncovered his thievery, and each time it felt like another blow to my stomach. *How could anyone do this?* The betrayal was a hard pill to swallow. He was a close friend; we hung out together, worked hard together — all for him to steal from right under my nose. Who does that to a friend? Disgusted and rattled to the core, something was telling me to get out of this business in a big way.

A Hard Lesson to Learn

They say that we don't learn lessons here on Earth when things are smooth and easy. Well, that was one hell of an experience. I'm sure my Spirit Guides were trying to tell me to get out of there. That nagging feeling that I had ignored for so long was them trying to tell me to get out, but it was too late. By the time I added up the amount he had stolen, I was financially devastated and had to shut down the business. I filed criminal theft charges against Roy and found myself under a mountain of paperwork preparing my case for the police department. I delivered a huge three-ringed binder of evidence to the detective.

"Wow," he said looking at the stack of evidence I brought in. "Typically, people just drop off a shoe box of papers and expect us to put it all together. I think I should hire you. I could use someone like you on my team. You should think about it."

I laughed at the comment, not giving it another thought. What I didn't realize at the time was that I was already on the path to law enforcement. The case went before the prosecutor, and Roy had to pay back the money he embezzled or face jail time. After the case was closed, the detective asked me again if I would be interested in a career in law enforcement. I told him I'd think about it and headed out the door.

With my mortgage business shut down and no source of income, I had to get creative. You'll never guess what I did next. I went back to what I knew best, and that was working with the animals. I placed an ad in the local paper as the "Corral Gal," and I scooped poop for a living. So, you see, I know the back end of a horse well. My livelihood depended on it.

At first, it was slow going. It was the onset of winter, and most people don't want their corral cleaned with snow on the ground. I had only a few clients, and it was back-breaking work. I also found a few pet-sitting and dog-walking jobs. Thankfully, my corral-cleaning side of the business started to flourish. I continued to add more clients who told their friends about my wonderful poop-scooping abilities, and my life got a whole lot easier thanks to manure.

Chapter 3:
Corral Gal

I have seen things so beautiful they have brought tears to my eyes.
Yet none of them can match the gracefulness and beauty of a horse running free.
~ Author Unknown

You are probably wondering what manure has to do with the afterlife. Well, hang in there; I'm getting to the good stuff. I did a lot of soul searching during my corral-cleaning days, and I began to feel a strong desire to give back to the community. That was unusual, as I had never volunteered for anything before. Being around animals every day was very fulfilling to me. I felt compelled to do something for animals, especially for those in need.

I'm sure all of this volunteering stuff was coming from my Spirit Guides, who were likely trying hard to get me to the next stage in my life. With their unyielding guidance, still, unbeknownst to me, I found my way to the Animal Control facility in Bailey, Colorado.

I walked into the cramped office one summer day and asked about volunteering. Before I could get the words out of my mouth, they put a shovel in one hand and bucket in the other. Another volunteer named Jeff led me to the back of the dilapidated facility and put me to work cleaning kennels.

As I became more familiar with procedures, I rode along with Alvin, the Animal Control Officer, and responded to animal-related calls. We rescued many neglected and abused animals together, and I began to feel a deep sense of belonging and kinship with the animals.

Law Enforcement Here I Come

One day, I was up to my elbows in dogs while cleaning kennels at the Animal Control facility when the sergeant approached me. I had been riding along with the deputies over the past few months and was beginning to feel like I knew what I was doing.

"I've heard some really good things about you," he said. "The other deputies tell me that you handle the calls really well."

I was surprised by the compliment. I thought most of my volunteer work went unnoticed by the higher-ranking officers we referred to as "The Brass."

"Thanks. I appreciate that." I looked down and realized I was covered from head to toe in dog hair. I tried to brush some of the hair off to no avail. What he said next just about floored me.

"You should consider becoming a full-time deputy. We need good people like you in this department."

Me? A cop? What? No way. He must be crazy. I had never even thought about becoming a cop. Never, never, never!

For the next few weeks, I couldn't stop thinking about what he said. *I must be crazy to even consider it*, I thought. Up until that moment, I had not even fired a gun. *Hmmm, I do enjoy the calls and handling the stressful situations. For all intents and purposes, I am doing the same job as the deputies I'm riding along with; I'm just not being paid for it. Maybe, just maybe, I could do this.*

Chapter 4:
Law Enforcement Stories

Dogs do speak, but only to those who know how to listen.
~ Orhan Pamuk

In the summer of 2000, I graduated from the Red Rocks Police Academy with the top award in Arrest Control. I was thirty-six years old. Not exactly a spring chicken. It was physically and emotionally exhausting at times, but I was ready for the challenge. It was not easy, but I was eager to accept my diploma on graduation day.

Karen and her mom, Ursula, on Graduation Day.

The Park County Sheriff's Office hired me in September of that same year, and I became the only female deputy in the department. I had to retire my pitchfork and muck boots, as now my job was "To Protect and Serve." *What in the world was I thinking?*

Connecting the Dots

The small sheriff's department did not have full coverage for staffing deputies around the clock, so I often worked alone. Responding to calls on my own, I became adept at reading people and their energy. My life depended on it. I had to arrive on a crime scene and, in a matter of minutes, determine what happened, who was lying, who was telling the truth, or who wanted to hurt me.

I watched subtle clues, such as the eye movements and the body language of suspects. I began to sense my intuition kicking in for my personal safety. As a rookie cop, everything started to come together for me for the first time.

I learned to trust my instincts when I sensed something wasn't right. Just like I sensed my former business partner was up to no good, I tuned into those feelings and paid attention to each case I worked on.

High up in the Rocky Mountains, I was experiencing an awakening of the spiritual kind. I began to remember long-forgotten senses and psychic abilities. I began to shed the layers of the material world that I had lived in for so long. I was shifting to a world of energy fields and sensory perception. Unknowingly, I was awakening my intuition to the psychic realm.

A Cat Finds the Suspect

It was during this time that I received my first message from my cat, Beeza. He told me he had a severe urinary blockage that turned out to be true. Here is an excerpt from my book *Hear All Creatures!*:

One Saturday morning I walked into the kitchen and saw Beeza lying on the floor. I walked over to the counter and said out loud, "Hi Beeza-Bee, how are you?"

Instantly I heard the words, "I'm blocked."

The words were in my own voice. I heard them very clearly, as though I had said them myself. But I hadn't. I was barely awake, and my mind was only set on making coffee.

I looked down at Beeza and said out loud, "Did you say that?"

"Yes. I'm blocked!" I again heard the words very clearly and urgently.

I took Beeza to the pet clinic, and his bladder was full. He was indeed blocked, and thankfully the doctor was able to successfully clear the blockage. That's when I realized that animals I encountered on a crime scene could be a wealth of information. I'll never forget the first time I got a message from a cat on a domestic violence call.

I was taking a statement from the female victim, while the two other officers searched the area for the suspect who fled on foot.

As I finished up the paperwork, a resident cat came out from behind a metal storage shed, looked right at me and then back at the shed, and said, "Inside."

No way; could the suspect be in that shed? Did the other deputies forget to search it? Could this cat tell me where the suspect was?

I approached the shed cautiously and ordered the suspect to come out with his hands up. Sure enough, the door slowly opened, and the suspect stepped out with his hands in the air. He was hiding in the shed right under our noses in a previously searched area. Had it not been for that cat, the suspect would have gotten away.

The Deer Pinpoint the Suspect's Location

On another night, a call came in for an armed suspect who fled the scene after losing control of his vehicle. I responded with lights and sirens blaring, along with two other officers. The sergeant ordered me to keep the perimeter around the vehicle secure. He and the other officer sped off down the road in search of the suspect.

Alone in the darkness, I scanned the area from a safe position behind a huge pine tree. As I listened to my fellow officers on my pack set, a portable walkie-talkie, I noticed a small herd of deer making their way through the grassy field. They knew I was there from their keen senses.

They dipped their heads down, eating the long grass, and kept a watchful eye on me. They knew I was not a threat and walked within several yards of my location. The other officers were about half a mile down the road and reported that they could not find the suspect. As the deer approached, I noticed they kept looking into the woods to my right. Even though all the police activity was to my left, they focused their eyes and ears to the right.

All of a sudden, the thought popped into my head, *Where is he hiding?*

It was just a thought in my mind, but I was looking directly at the deer. In an instant, I heard, "Logs, behind the logs," and then saw the image of a fallen tree flash through my mind. It was just like my own thought, only it wasn't my thought. I wasn't thinking about a log. I was thinking, *What in the hell am I gonna do if I find this guy?*

I drew my weapon and swept back silently through the darkness out of sight. Just ahead, I could see several fallen logs in the grass. My heart was pounding in my chest as I approached. I could feel the suspect's energy radiating out of the woods.

"Sheriff's Office! Show me your hands!" I ordered.

I don't know where the words came from, but they poured out of my mouth with such a command presence it surprised even me.

"Show me your hands NOW!" I bellowed.

Then the most incredible thing happened. Out from the grass two human hands came up like Pop-Tarts out of a toaster.

A pleading voice said, "Don't shoot! Don't shoot!"

I quickly radioed that I had the suspect at gunpoint. The deer had long since disappeared into the darkness. I handcuffed the suspect and placed him in the backseat of my patrol car.

The other officers flew over to my location at lightning speed, gave me high-fives, and patted me on the back.

"Way to go, Anderson!" the sergeant said. "Good work. How did you know where he was?"

Um, I'll never tell.

Chapter 5:
Animals on Crime Scenes

Clearly, animals know more than we think
and think a great deal more than we know.
~ *Dr. Irene M. Pepperberg, Ph.D.*

O nce I began my career in law enforcement, it didn't take long for the animals to prove to be good eyewitnesses. Animals are honest, unbiased and would show me exactly what happened. There were many times that I obtained information from them on case investigations; I just never told anyone my confidential informants had four legs and a tail.

In one case, a family's dog told me which direction to look when a missing boy vanished into the National Forest. A few hours later, the Search and Rescue team found the boy unharmed in the area the dog indicated.

During a call for domestic violence, a cat told me that the aggressor was the woman, not the man. At first, it appeared the woman was the victim, as she had cuts and red marks on her arms. It was later confirmed that she cut herself to make it look like her husband hit her.

A Man With a Gun

I responded to 911 call, and when I arrived on the scene, I saw a man covered with blood waving a gun in the air. He claimed he was attacked by his neighbor's dogs.

I asked him what happened, and he told me an elaborate story that didn't make sense. His own dogs were in the house, so I silently asked them what happened. His dogs told me that the man was the aggressor and that he violently attacked the other dogs.

Apparently, he got fed up when the neighbor's dogs pooped in his yard. In frustration, he chased after them and hit them repeatedly with a shovel. In the scuffle, the dogs knocked him to the ground and attacked him.

Thank goodness a witness verified the events, so I didn't have to write a report that said, *I interviewed the dogs, and they confirmed the man was guilty.*

An Old Hound Dog

A report of an unattended death of an elderly man came over the radio one day. You never know if an unattended death is a homicide, suicide or natural death, so extreme caution has to be taken to preserve the scene.

The paramedics had already tended to the victim, but it was too late. The man was dead. The house was in shambles with furniture knocked over and items scattered all over the floor. Based on what I saw, someone must have brutally attacked this old man.

As I put up the crime scene tape, I noticed an old hound dog waiting patiently on the back porch. He seemed to be oblivious to all the commotion and kept his eyes on the screen door. I could sense the dog's hunger, so I got some dog treats out of my patrol car, which he gulped down.

As I waited for the Animal Control Officer to respond, I asked the dog what happened. The dog told me that this man was alone in the house and started to cry out in pain. The old dog said there were loud crashing sounds and then silence. He said his human never came outside again. I thought the dog had to be wrong, because the house was such a mess.

The Victim Died From a Massive Seizure

The coroner later concluded that the old man was a victim of a severe epileptic attack, as he failed to take his prescribed medication. His violent episodes knocked over the furniture so it looked like there was a fight.

The old hound dog was right. After that incident, I realized that the animals could provide accurate details of an event as seen through their own eyes. Those cases were the stepping stones that eventually led me to my work as a psychic and a medium.

Chapter 6:
From Deputy to Psychic

Until one has loved an animal,
a part of one's soul remains unawakened.
~ Anatole France

Several years later, I decided to leave law enforcement and move to the Spokane, Washington, area. It was a tough decision, as I loved being a cop, but the suspects were getting younger and I was getting older. I knew I would not pursue law enforcement in the Spokane area, so I went back to what I knew best. And no, it wasn't manure this time. I found work back in the mortgage industry again.

My Life Was Unraveling

It was a strange and unsettling time. No matter how hard I tried, I could not get any insight into what was ahead for me. I felt as if I was in a void and couldn't shake it off. I was trudging through the days working at a job I did not like. Even the one thing that used to bring me so much joy, connecting with animals, was beginning to wear me down.

I was conducting animal communication sessions part-time to sharpen my skills, when I began to sense that many people had negative feelings about my psychic work. Several friends accused me of being evil and practicing witchcraft. Those remarks were very hurtful and upsetting.

Nothing seemed to be going right. I hated my job, my relationship was unraveling, and the few friends I had thought I was a witch. Great, my life was officially falling apart.

Just when I felt like I was at the bottom of the barrel of life, I was invited to attend a barbecue in Spokane on the 4th of July.

Up until that day, I had lost my direction and forgotten my purpose in life. This is where my first book, *Hear All Creatures!*, comes into play once more. I met a little white dove at that party. His messages helped me understand how important it was for me to continue my path as an animal communicator. That pivotal moment changed everything for me.

Here is an excerpt from the book:

We were sitting in the shade on a deck, when the host of the party asked if I wanted to go see the neighbor's wild bird. Apparently, this lucky little guy had been rescued from the mouths of one of her cats, and they were nursing it back to health. Knowing how much I loved animals and that I knew how to communicate with them, Terri, the next-door neighbor, had invited me over for a look.

Several of us trotted next door, and a few moments later, Terri came out with a beautiful white dove on her index finger.

As I listened to Terri explain how she had rescued the bird from those feline jaws, I extended my finger to this quiet, calm, little dove. To my amazement, he stepped easily onto my finger without hesitation. He sat perfectly still, even while several children ran through the room asking to pet him.

"Ask him if he likes his food!" one little boy yelled.

"And if he likes his cage!" another excited little boy added.

The whole family gathered near me to hear what this little dove had to say. Silently, I said my blessing and prayer and asked his permission to communicate.

To my surprise, the dove cocked his head at me and mentally replied, "I've been expecting you."

"What's he saying? What's he saying?" cried the children, almost in unison.

"Indeed," he said calmly. "The human who talks to animals," he added in a very matter of fact voice. "I've been expecting you. Tell them the food is fine, but please keep the cats away from the cage. I would also like to be up higher."

I repeated to the group what the dove said about his food. Terri confirmed that the dove was being kept in a dog crate on the floor and that the cats could get their paws inside. I wasn't sure what he meant by, "I've been expecting you," so I just kept quiet about that.

"He doesn't want the cats near him. Perhaps you can raise his cage," I suggested, returning my attention to the dove.

"Where did he come from?" one boy asked. "From up above," the dove answered quietly.

"Did he come from a family? Does he want to go home?"

The questions were being fired at me one after the other.

"I come from Heaven above. I am here to meet with you. I have been waiting for this moment," he said to me as he sat quietly perched on the end of my index finger.

Suddenly, I felt a rush. Not wind, but something more internal. The family's questions drifted away, and I could hear only the dove as he spoke directly to me.

Looking directly at me, he declared, "I am here to tell you to follow your heart, follow your path, my child. I am here for you; it is your calling. You know it in your heart. You know the right thing to do."

"What's he saying? What's his name?" the questions from the children kept on coming, but I couldn't take my eyes off the dove.

"You have come up against adversity and negativity," he stated.

At that moment, I remembered the hurtful comments I had experienced. Tears poured from my eyes — not tears of pain but of understanding.

"You have been getting away from this lately, haven't you?" the dove asked.

"Well, yes, I have," I answered telepathically. I realized that the recent events of my life were unfolding like a mini-movie in my mind. I saw myself from a strange perspective, almost as though I was watching the past happen again. I sensed my own fears and doubts resurfacing; I felt the sting of pain as my friends made rude comments about my communication skills.

"My child, have you ever been touched by the hand of God?" the little white dove asked. I could feel the warmth of his feet flowing down my hand into my arm; it felt peaceful and comforting.

"Well, I don't think so. I think I would remember that," I stammered back, not quite knowing how to answer.

"Consider yourself touched by His hand," he said. "You are a child of God. You know in your heart you must continue your work. Fear not, my child, it is your purpose in this lifetime."

I stood in total awe of what seemed like to be an eternity. The children were anxiously awaiting the dove's answers, but I couldn't speak. I didn't know how to tell them that his messages were meant for me.

"Ask him what he wants his name to be," one of the children demanded, getting impatient with me, as I had been silent for too long.

"Tell them I would like a name with dignity," the dove said.

"He would like a name with dignity," I stammered, trying to regain my composure. I would find out later that the family had named him Noah. He is with them to this day, in his lovely cage high above the cats.

At the exact moment when I needed him the most, the Universe brought Noah to me that day, and it made all difference in the world.

Energy Flows Where Attention Goes

It's all so obvious now, as I look back to those troubled times. When things are not going right, when you are hit time and time again with obstacles, it's likely the Universe trying to tell you that you are on the wrong path. I could not have been more disconnected from my gifts, my needs and myself as I was at that time.

There is a saying that *energy flows where attention goes*, and all my energy was going in the wrong direction. I had become buried under the stress from life and lost my way. I had forgotten who I was and what I was doing. Along with all of that, I had stopped communicating with animals. I was putting everyone's needs before my own. It was time to make a change.

A Renewed Sense of Self

After the messages I received from Noah the dove, I began to refocus my energy. I put all my attention back into myself and started honoring my gifts as an animal communicator. I was now priority number one; nobody else, just me. I had a renewed sense of self, and I felt alive again for the first time in a long time.

It took an enormous leap of faith, but I walked away from a high-paying corporate job. It was the best thing I ever did. After that, things just started to fall into place.

I started teaching classes and began conducting sessions at psychic shows and expos, and new clients were rolling in. The wheels were in motion, and the Universe was smiling down upon me. I was back on track, all thanks to a little white dove.

Chapter 7:
I'm a Psychic and a Medium

How it is that animals understand things I do not know,
but it is certain that they do understand.
~ Frances Hodgson Burnett

I consider myself a psychic and a medium. A psychic is someone who can sense things about people and situations that goes far beyond the five senses. A medium is someone who can communicate with departed souls. Not all psychics are mediums, and not all mediums are psychic. I just happen to be both.

As a psychic, I rely on all of my senses to obtain information for my clients. The five most common sensory perceptions are known as sight, hearing, taste, smell and touch.

As a medium, I have the ability to receive messages from both departed animals and departed human beings. I connect with them in a very straightforward way of communication, just like how you and I would connect on a phone call.

There are also extra senses, sometimes referred to as our sixth sense, which can access even more detailed psychic information. Among these extra senses are the five "clairs."

The Five Clairs

The five main *clairs* are known as clairvoyance, clairaudience, claircognizance, clairsentience and clairalience. Most psychics rely on these extrasensory perceptions for their work. One *clair* is not necessarily better than another, and these abilities may shift or expand with time. Pay attention to how you receive information to determine your most dominant *clair*.

Clairvoyance — Clear Seeing

Clairvoyance is when you see images flash through your mind, much like a daydream, of things you shouldn't otherwise know about.

Clairaudience — Clear Hearing

Being clairaudient is when you hear words, sounds or thoughts in your mind, in your own voice, but you know they aren't your thoughts. Psychic sounds and spirit communication can also come through in someone else's voice.

Claircognizance — Clear Knowing

Claircognizance is when you sense things about people or events that you would not normally know. Premonitions or a strange, unsettling feeling that something is about to happen is an example of claircognizance.

Clairsentience — Clear Feeling

If you feel another person's emotions or physical pain, that is called clairsentience. Empaths or those naturally sensitive to emotions are likely clairsentient.

Clairalience — Clear Smelling

If you have ever caught the scent of a deceased loved one's perfume, cigar or cigarette smoke, that is called clairalience. When there is no natural source to produce these smells, it is our psychic abilities tuning into a spirit's presence.

Clairgustance — Clear Tasting

This is the one clair I try to avoid when I'm working with animals. I don't need to know what it tastes like when a dog gets into the trash. A cat shared the taste of a mouse with me one time. Needless to say, now I make sure that never happens again.

Each of us has the ability to tune into our extra senses. Over time, you can sharpen one or all of your senses. It is merely a matter of practicing and paying attention to how you receive incoming information.

Smudgie

During a session with a deceased cat named Smudgie, I was able to utilize almost all of the clairs to see, hear and feel specific messages from this sweet kitty. Smudgie told me to say the word *marshmallows*; then she flashed an image of a box or a special delivery. And, finally, she sent an overwhelming feeling of excitement and joy.

Smudgie

When I asked her mom, Emma, what the marshmallows and the special delivery were all about, Emma laughed out loud and confessed that she was so excited because she had just special ordered a certain flavor of Peeps, the marshmallow treats for Easter.

We were both stunned by the detailed messages. Smudgie was obviously right there when her mom ordered the Peeps, and sure enough, the box of treats was delivered the next day.

Chapter 8:
Telepathy;
The Foundation of
Animal Communication

You don't know what mental telepathy exists
from the human to the animal.
~ Tippi Hedren

Communicating with an animal, living or deceased, is primarily based on telepathy or mind-to-mind communication. Telepathy is a way of communicating thoughts directly from one mind to another without speech or physical signs. Messages are sent and received using extrasensory means. There is also a bit of quantum physics involved along with the forces of matter and energy. To keep things simple, think about it this way: You don't need to know how the engine works in your car to drive it. Nor do you need to know how your cell phone works to make a phone call.

The same applies to animal communication. You don't need to know how it works from a scientific standpoint. You just need to trust that it works. I encourage you to research telepathy and quantum physics in greater detail to learn more about these fascinating topics. But for now, I'll just keep it simple.

51

Create a Loving Space for Welcoming Souls

I create the perfect atmosphere to conduct a session through meditation. Meditating creates a loving space filled with peace and gratitude that is inviting and welcoming for everyone involved. I need the animal's energy to be near me so I can see, hear or feel them.

The animal's energy comes through surrounded by a sphere of White Light. This luminous, protective shield emanates from God, our Divine Creator. It is a powerful, glowing energy that keeps all energies separate and safe during sessions.

I can sense the animal energies lining up, much like how planes line up in a flight pattern as they approach the airport. I often feel like an air traffic controller trying to keep each animal's messages separate as other spirits start to come through. Animals don't have to come through if they don't want to, but most of the time they are eager to communicate.

They can manifest in partial form or full form. Sometimes they look just like they were here on Earth. Other times, I don't see them at all; I just sense them. Many times I'll feel the nose of a dog bump my arm, a cat rub up against my leg, or a horse stomp its feet. Since I connect with a photo of the animal, they may not feel the need to manifest in full form. Each pet is unique, and some would rather conserve their energy for other things, such as sending messages.

I have only had a few cases when I've had to coax an animal to share a message. In those cases, the pet was either scared, lost or seriously injured. Usually, they are excited to share their loving messages with you.

Chapter 9:
How Animal Communication Works

Energy cannot be created or destroyed;
it can only be changed from one form to another.
~ Albert Einstein

There are a few different methods of connecting with a departed pet. Some people connect during a shamanic journey, which is an ancient form of shifting consciousness by using rhythmic drumming or rattles. Others may connect with the help of their Spirit Guides or through meditation. It is all a matter of preference or training, and one method is not necessarily better than the next. We all receive psychic information differently, so it depends on how we receive the clearest incoming information.

As I mentioned earlier, I use a photograph to make the connection with a departed animal. Using a photo, I can dial up a pet's energy just like dialing their cell phone number. A photo isn't always necessary, as sometimes a pet will just appear and join us in a session. Other times a description is all I need to make the connection.

As a psychic, I read energy. This energy is all around us, and it's what makes the world go around. An animal's soul, or their energy, contains all of their life experiences while they were here on Earth, as well as all their past life memories.

When the animal's soul leaves their physical body at the brink of death, I refer to this event as crossing over — as they cross over from our Earthly dimension into the spirit realm. The soul leaves the body behind and transitions into a new existence as an energetic being.

It is actually easier for me to connect with a deceased animal compared to a living animal, as there is no physical body to interfere with the messages. Departed animals are pure energy, and with fewer physical distractions, connecting is instantaneous.

Animals Send Messages as Pictures

Animals will often send images to convey a thought or a message. Those images can vary and include everything from a favorite toy to a person or a special place. *If they can see it, they can send it.*

For example, think about your favorite food. Picture what it looks like. Is it a piece of cake or ice cream? Maybe it's a bowl of spaghetti. You can probably see it in your mind even though you are reading this page. Notice how the image that flashed in your mind fades as you redirected your focus back to this book.

That is how animals send pictures or images. It happens with lightning speed and can disappear just as fast. By paying attention to the images, I can describe what I am seeing and convey the message to the client.

Brie and the Tape Measure

A deceased cat named Brie sent an image of a tape measure as I was waiting for her mom, Rachel, to call in for her session. I was a bit confused by the image, so I asked Rachel what that tape measure meant to her.

Apparently, just before the session, Rachel was measuring her mattress so she could get the right-sized sheets. While using the tape measure, she saw Brie's favorite pillow on the bed and immediately thought about her beautiful cat and how much she missed her. Brie picked up on her mom's thoughts and sent me the image of the tape measure. What a wonderful way for Brie to let her mom know she was right there on her favorite pillow watching her measure the bed.

In addition to images, animals can also send a thought or moving pictures. It is like watching a video of an event or a situation in my mind.

Imagine walking into one of those warehouse television stores that have all the screens flashing big, bright images. Some images make sense right away, but there are some images I don't understand. I will often see things from the animal's perspective. Since most pets are much lower to the ground than we are, they send images of their vantage point. Once I describe what their pets are showing me, my clients can usually determine what the message means to them.

How Animals Send Human Words

Learning the language of the animals is just like learning a new human language. When you go to a foreign country and are not fluent in the language, you have to learn what each word means. The translation process can be slow and tedious, as you have to look up each word one by one. The more time you spend in that country, the more fluent you become.

With practice, the translation process becomes easier, and the new words begin to pop into your mind. Your memory stores the new words and symbols you've learned, and you can draw from that stored memory and begin to translate words and sentences more quickly. The same process applies to learning how to understand animals.

When an animal sends a message, it contains an energetic property or an impression. That impression, which is just like a thought, is sent to me telepathically — similar to an email message.

Distance and Time Are Not Barriers

Distance and time are not barriers, so energetic messages can be received instantly across many miles. Once I receive that message, I can translate the impression based on my stored memory and symbols. Since I can hear with my internal psychic ear, the messages are translated into sounds, words or sentences that I understand. The translation process develops over time with practice.

How Can Animals Speak English?

Well, that's all fine and dandy for learning a human language, but animals don't speak English. How can they send human words? Simply said, a translation process occurs because I have developed a relationship with my Spirit Guides, and they present the messages to me in a format that I understand.

Spirit Guides are discarnate beings that watch over us and help us navigate through our lifetime. We all have Spirit Guides, even if you are not aware of their presence. Some Spirit Guides are assigned to us before we are born and stay with us until we die. Others are temporary and join us when a particular situation presents itself. I have three main Spirit Guides whom I work with, and each one has a different task or specialty to help me connect with the animals.

Miki the Cat From Japan

Many years ago, a client from Japan named Kyoko contacted me when her cat, Miki, went missing. I was surprised when the cat's messages came through in English. I am not fluent in the Japanese language, and I did not know until that moment if I would be able to understand Miki's messages. Because of the translation process, my Spirit Guides sent the messages using my symbols and in my frame of reference. I was able to understand every word, and Miki was found a few blocks away.

Murungu

When animals don't know how to explain something, they will send images of the message they want to convey. Such was the case with Murungu, a fourteen-year-old Great Dane mix. Shortly after he crossed over, Murungu's energy came through with his owner Diana's parents, who were also on the Other Side.

Murungu

Diana was elated to hear that her parents greeted him when he crossed over. During the session, Murungu told me to talk about his towel or blanket and said it was in a special place. He wasn't able to describe where it was, so he showed me a car. Diana confirmed that she made a car seat cover out of his blanket so he will always be with her, even when she is driving. Murungu also asked me to mention a bench. Diana just happened to be sitting on a bench in her sunroom during our call.

Animals Send Emotions

Emotions are one of the most common ways that animals convey a message. Whether they are living or deceased, animals can send an energetic message containing different feelings. An example of the power of emotions would be if you have ever walked into a room after someone was arguing; the air can be so thick you can cut it with a knife. Even though the argument has ended, the emotional energy remains.

Emotions Erupted

During one of my Animal Communication workshops in North Carolina, a woman named Barbara was practicing her communication skills with a deceased cat named Vito. She suddenly broke into tears and could not stop crying. Flustered and emotional, she explained she felt a sense of abandonment but could not tell us why. She said the powerful emotions washed over her in waves. The cat's owner, Leon, explained what happened.

He and his wife were in the military and deployed overseas. They could not take Vito with them, and they were devastated, as they loved him like a human child. A friend took the cat, and sadly, they left Vito behind. Leon said they grieved as if they had lost a child.

About a month later, Vito bolted out the door and disappeared. He was never found, and Leon had no idea what happened to him. They never resolved their grief and still held onto that sorrow as if it just happened.

Once I heard what happened, I opened up a space for the cat's energy to join us. I explained to Vito what happened and why his humans left him so many years ago. Leon was finally able to express his feelings and devotion to his beloved cat.

Within minutes, the healing process began, and the air around us became lighter and calmer. The emotionally charged atmosphere softened, and I watched both Leon and Vito move from a painful memory into a peaceful place.

Barbara picked up on Vito's emotions but could not determine what the cause was. By opening up the lines of communication, everyone involved was able to understand what happened. The pain was gone. The magical healing effects of communicating with animals never cease to amaze me.

Chapter 10:
Hearing and Seeing Animal Spirits

An animal's eyes have the power to speak a great language.
~ Martin Bube

When I first began my career as an Animal Communicator, I learned primarily on my own. I studied animal behavior and read every book I could find on psychic development. That's right about the time I discovered the famous psychic John Edward. I recorded every episode of his television show *Crossing Over* and watched them over and over again.

I learned a lot by watching John's techniques and listening to his style of delivering messages. Since John is primarily clairaudient, meaning he can hear the spirits talking, I formed my style around that method. My main goal was to be able to hear the animals speak, so with practice, I developed a strong psychic ear.

Many years ago, I was conducting a gallery reading at a psychic expo in Spokane when a woman in the audience named Kacy showed me a picture of her dog, Bella. As soon as I looked at Bella's photo, I heard the dog say, "Nervous, nervous, nervous!" When I shared this message with Kacy, she said that Bella suffered from extreme anxiety and that described her perfectly.

Soon I began to hear all the animals speaking to me, and that's when I wrote my book *Hear All Creatures!*, as I could literally hear them.

My dear friend Ron had a Jack Russell, named Jilly, that crossed over at the age of sixteen. During one of our many sessions, Jilly told me to talk about spiral circles, some bones and a spear. Of course, none of this made any sense to me, but I told Ron what Jilly said, and he could barely contain his shock. He sent me this note:

Jilly

"After Jilly had died, I made a Celtic spiral in the backyard with concentric circles," he explained. "I put her remains (her ashes/bones) in the center, and last but not least I placed a very powerful spear in the center of the spiral. Karen, the only one who knows this is my wife."

Jilly described it perfectly down to her last detail even though it happened after she died.

Another time, I was driving into town and talking to Ron on my Bluetooth. He had just completed a shamanic journey and visited Jilly on the Other Side. A shamanic journey is when part of the soul is free to leave the body during a meditative journey to heal or visit another soul in another dimension. During that visit, Ron gave her a gift. He asked me if Jilly could show me that gift.

"Ron, I'm driving right now. I can check in when I get back home." Then, suddenly, I saw Jilly pushing a red ball with her nose.

"Okay, wait one minute; Jilly says you gave her a red ball as a gift," I said, thinking to myself that there is probably a law out there somewhere that says it is against the law to drive while communicating with animals.

"That is incredible!" he said. "You can see what I gave Jilly during one of my journeys. Wow, that's impressive."

After that, it was just a matter of time before the animal spirits started to appear before me. Once I gazed into their eyes, it was like opening up the pages of their life.

Every so often an animal's spirit would show up in the most unusual place. I was at the grocery store one day, when I saw the spirit of a crow hopping around on a man's shoulder. The man had no idea the bird was following him. I glanced in his cart and saw a bag of wild bird seed. I felt the love the bird had for the man, and I couldn't help but smile as he walked by.

He thought I was flirting with him, as he immediately struck up a conversation with me. I didn't have the heart to tell him I was smiling at the spirit of his crow, not him.

Another time I was getting my hair cut, when I saw the spirit of a cat circling around the feet of another patron. I started chatting with the woman, and she told me her elderly cat had recently passed away.

Our departed pets like to spend time with us and are never more than a thought away. When they aren't around us, just imagine them galavanting around the cosmos in the love-filled effervescence of the afterlife.

Part II

Part II

Chapter 11:
The Other Side

There is no death. Only a change of worlds.
~ Chief Seattle

What Is the Other Side?

The Other Side is where our animal's energy exists after their physical body dies. It is another dimension — also referred to as Heaven or Eternity — that overlaps our atmosphere. Once an animal leaves its body, there are many different entry and exit points, called portals, through which their energy, or soul, travel between Earth and the Other Side.

The animals tell me they can appear just about anywhere here on Earth. They can move back and forth between our dimension and theirs with ease. Their favorite entry point is usually in familiar territories, such as their favorite bed, chair or windowsill. Some like to re-enter through outside portals in the yard, such as a field, the barn or any other place that they spent a lot of time.

Where Is the Other Side?

As you're sitting in your chair reading this book, put your arm out in front of you. Your arm is now on the Other Side. Now, reach down toward your foot. That foot and that hand are on the Other Side. It's not some far-away Universe or miles above us. It's right here — all around us.

The overlapping of this other world or dimension is what allows our departed pets to interact with us after their physical death. Some speculate that the Other Side is about two or three feet off the ground, which would explain why some apparitions appear to be floating in the air.

Some animal spirits appear to me at ground level, near my feet or jumping in my lap, while others seem to float and hover in the thin air. Just like our pets, *we are all spiritual beings having a physical experience on Earth*. One day, when our time on Earth ends, we will move into other dimensions just as our pets have done before us.

According to the animals, the Other Side is a comfortable, loving, joyous space that encompasses the same areas they enjoyed in physical form. The main difference is now the animal's spirit, or energy, can go anywhere they want. A fence, a yard or the walls of a house no longer restrict their movement.

Tangerine the Cat

I've had sessions where deceased animals are with their humans at work, in the car, on vacation and many other unusual places. A deceased cat named Tangerine told me to say the word "toothpaste" when I opened up his photo before a session one day.

"Toothpaste?" I asked the orange tabby. "Okay. I'll talk about toothpaste."

Sometimes crazy messages come through that don't make sense to me, but it's my job to deliver the message. No matter how strange, funny or sad, I am simply the messenger and share whatever comes through. So when Tangerine's human mom, Cathy, called in, I told her what Tangerine said.

"I'm not sure why, but I'm supposed to talk about toothpaste. What does that reference mean to you?" I asked.

"I can't believe you're saying that. I was just at the store today and bought a tube of toothpaste. That's all I bought. Was Tangerine at the store with me?"

"Yes, indeed! He saw what you were buying and wanted to let you know he is still around you."

Cathy started to cry, but they were tears of happiness. "I've been missing him so much. He was my world, my everything. I was standing in line buying the toothpaste thinking about him because the man in front of me was buying cat food. That's amazing that he was right there with me!"

Many clients often tell me they have felt, or sensed, their departed pet around them. Some report that they saw their beloved pet out of the corner of their eye or felt them jump on the bed. These things truly happen, and our pets can visit us any time.

"Talk about the round, glittery thing," a deceased Maltese named Buddy said during his session.

"What is this?" I asked the dog, not quite sure what he was showing me.

"I don't know, but it catches the light," he said, as I saw a round, sparkly globe flash across my mind.

As it turned out, his mom, Barbara, had a disco ball hanging from the ceiling in her office. I love it when animals share something they see right at that moment. I also kept seeing the color blue around Buddy. Barbara told me she keeps his favorite blue blanket on his doggie bed next to her desk.

Munchkin and the Crumpets

Even though that sounds like the name of a band, it actually involved a session with a deceased dog named Munchkin.

"Talk about crumpets," came the odd message from the deceased dachshund.

I had no idea how much that message would mean to Munchkin's mom, Darleen.

Darleen was puzzled. "Wow, how can he know that?"

"Do you eat crumpets?" I asked, not even sure what they were. I knew the British liked them, but what a strange reference for the dog to send to me.

"I had crumpets this morning for breakfast. They are like English muffins. I've never had them before, but they were a gift from a friend. Munchkin was a total chowhound, and I thought of him as I was eating them. It made me sad to think he may never find me in my new home."

Darleen had been mourning the loss of her sweet boy for months and could not sense the little dog's energy around her. She was worried that Munchkin wouldn't be able to find her due to a recent move across several states.

"I've felt so guilty for moving," Darleen said. "We buried him in the backyard and then found out we had to relocate for my husband's job. It felt like we were abandoning him. I haven't done anything but cry and mope around the new house. I haven't even met any of the neighbors."

"Well, worry no more. Munchkin had no problem finding you, and now you have a full-time breakfast companion!" I smiled through the phone.

I received a card from Darleen several weeks later telling me how renewed she felt now that she knew Munchkin was with her. Her whole outlook on life changed dramatically since she heard that one little message. She started socializing with her new neighbors, joined a grief recovery group and started volunteering at a local animal shelter.

"I feel like I can breathe again, Karen. Thank you for giving me back my life."

I am always honored to hear things like that, but all the credit goes to the animals. I'm merely the messenger. Who could know that one little message could be so healing?

What Is it Like on the Other Side?

Animals tell me that the Other Side is a loving, joyful space, surrounded by souls that honor them and care about them. Most of the time, our departed pets are with our personal soul group, consisting of family, friends and loved ones — both human and animal. There are some instances when animals will come through with an angelic being, Archangels, Spirit Guides, or other people and animals that you do not know.

It feels wonderful to be in this space with them. Imagine floating effortlessly in a lagoon of warm, crystal clear water. The temperature is just right, about 76–80 degrees, the air smells fresh and clean, and a calm breeze softly blows. No aches or pains exist as they did in the physical world. Without a body to restrict them, the animals travel back and forth through dimensions with ease, hanging out in favorite spots as they would in life. They can be in more than one place at one time and, again, are not bound by physical limitations.

"I feel fantastic!" said a recently deceased cat named Boo Boo. "I can fly!" And with that, I saw the energy of the silky black cat whisk playfully around my office.

Animals will often speak joyfully and gleefully about their life here on Earth and rarely want to delve into anything painful or uncomfortable. Their favorite topic is themselves, and their next favorite subject is, well, themselves.

They will also share information about their home, their human caretakers, and other little interesting tidbits. They like to talk about things that are important to them, and the range of topics varies with each animal.

During one session, a deceased dog named Leo kept dropping a tennis ball at my feet, staring at me and waiting for me to throw it. His mom, Katherine, said that was his favorite game when he was alive.

Just think about what your pet loved to do when they were alive, and that is likely what they are doing on the Other Side.

Does My Pet Miss Me?

I'm often asked if a pet misses their humans after they cross over, and I'm sorry to say the answer is no, but let me explain why. Your departed animals are never far from you and continue to be a part of your life. Not much changes for them when they cross over to the Other Side.

They are still able to see you and love you, so they rarely say they miss you. It may be difficult to hear that, but try not to get your feelings hurt. It's actually a good thing because that means they are still around you.

Will My Pet Be Jealous if I Adopt a New Animal?

Many times, a client will ask if their departed pet will be jealous or angry with them for getting another pet. In most cases, the answer is no. Your animals want you to enjoy your life to the fullest. When you express love toward another animal, your departed pet can feel that love too.

Animals also have the ability to let go of anything that does not serve them. They rarely hold a grudge or speak ill of their human or other animals. Occasionally, I'll hear about sibling rivalry or perhaps a clash between resident pets, but for the most part, they will refer to it, and then they let it go.

Unlike humans, animals don't like to rehash old wounds or difficult times. Most departed pets are genuinely happy and feeling good whenever I check in on them.

Can My Pet See Me?

The animals tell me that when they cross over to the Other Side, they see us as glowing orbs of light. In their mind's eye, we still look the same to them based on their memories; our vibrational energy makes us recognizable.

For example, watch an animal react when their human puts a mask over their face. The animal won't recognize the mask, but as soon as they hear or smell their human, they suddenly know who it is even with the mask on. Our aura, or the energy around us, and our unique vibrational structure is as recognizable to them as our faces. No matter where we are in this world, our pets can pick up on our unique energetic imprint.

Animals can also see and feel their surroundings just as they did when they were alive. That's why you may see or feel their energy zipping around the house just as they did when they were alive and well.

A deceased golden retriever named Winchester told us during a session one day that his mom and dad's energy glowed like a brilliantly lit light bulb when they were happy. He described seeing bright light around the center of their chest, heart and faces.

Who Do Animals See on the Other Side?

Animals see other spirits on the Other Side the same way they used to see us when they were alive. They can also feel and sense the energy of the person or familiar places.

Almost everything happens telepathically on the Other Side. When you want to be with someone, you are instantly around them. If you want to go to the beach, you are there in the blink of an eye. They can also feel and sense the energy of other people, animals or familiar places.

Our pets can still see us, but since they don't have a physical body anymore, they don't see with their eyes. They sense things or see things with their energy.

Think about standing in line at the grocery store. Your eyes are looking forward, but you can sense someone behind you in line. You can feel them in your space. You don't have to turn around to see the person; you sense their energy near you. The same applies to how our pets sense us from the Other Side.

How Do Our Pets Communicate on the Other Side?

Communicating with souls on the Other Side is similar to how we communicate in our dreams. Notice how you don't have to speak in your dreams. Your thoughts are all you need to accomplish whatever you want. When a loved one is in your dreams, you don't necessarily recognize their face, but you sense their energy, and you immediately know each other.

We can do just about anything in a dream. We can fly like a bird or swim underwater without needing oxygen. All of this is just like being on the Other Side. When I communicate with a deceased animal, I am primarily clairaudient, meaning I hear their words. However, some animals are better at sending images, and others are better at conveying emotions. Some pets use all of those methods when they communicate with me, so I have to modify my abilities and raise my vibration to fit each individual animal.

Some pets are really good at sending messages, while others aren't. It is similar to talking to a person. Some people are really good communicators, while others aren't. Some people will express themselves with a lot of emotion or gestures, and others will be more reserved.

The animals are the same way. I have to prepare for just about anything during a session, including the clients themselves. I'm also working with their energy, and sometimes it can make or break a session.

Be sure you bring calm, positive energy to any psychic or animal communication session. If you're not up to it, distracted or not feeling well, it is best to reschedule. Bringing positive energy to a session will make the lines of communication open up for the best session possible.

Are Our Pets Always Around Us After They Die?

After your pet crosses over, they tend to stay close by, keeping an eye on you and hanging around in their favorite places. You may feel them near you and sense their loving energy very strongly around your home. As time goes by, their energy may not feel as intense as it once was.

There are several reasons for this. Your pets continue to learn and grow as energetic beings after they cross over. As their soul evolves, some will participate in different activities in the afterlife. These activities may include helping other humans and animals cross over or preparing to reincarnate and return to Earth. Other pets may merge with a group consciousness.

Their spiritual path may take them into other parts of the world or even into other Universes, depending on what their journey as a spiritual being consists of. The longer your pet has been on the Other Side, the more transparent they become to you here on Earth. Each soul is unique and stays connected to you while they follow their perfect and divine path.

Can You Still Talk to Them if They Have Reincarnated?

Some psychics believe that you cannot communicate with a pet if they have reincarnated, because they are now in another body living another life. Yet, others say it is possible to connect with that soul. I'll go into more detail about this later in the chapter about reincarnation, but for now, I'll tell you that I can connect with any animal at any time regardless of the status of reincarnation. Maybe that's just my style, but I've never had a problem connecting with either the animal soul you remember or the newly reincarnated soul.

I've been asked if there is a time frame as to how far back I can go to connect with a childhood pet. I have yet to find a limit. I have a few clients that are in their 90s, and I can easily connect with any of their departed pets.

Chapter 12:
Signs From the Afterlife

Your loved ones are just a thought away.
~ John Holland

This is one of my favorite topics. There are so many different signs from the afterlife, it boggles the mind. After your pet crosses over, they will often try to let you know they are still around you. Sometimes they will appear vividly in your dreams, and other times they may brush up against you just as they did when they were alive. Not everyone can feel or sense their pet's energy, but most will tell me they are never more than a thought away.

"Why can't I feel my dog's spirit around me?" asked Jesse, after he lost his 13-year-old pit bull mix, named Axel.

Axel looked at me with the saddest eyes. "I'm never far away," the dog said. "Tell him I'm here." And with that, he showed me an alarm clock.

"I see an alarm clock, Jesse; does that make sense to you? Why would Axel show me that?"

Jesse told me that just about every weekend since Axel died, his alarm clock goes off at 5:30 a.m. all by itself.

"Oh my gosh; that's Axel? We used to go for an early morning jog on the weekends," Jesse said. "I wondered if he had something to do with that."

An Animal's Energy Can Manipulate Electronics

It takes a lot of energy for animals to manifest in any form. I explained to Jesse that Axel was manipulating his electronic equipment because it's easy for him to do that.

"Axel is pure energy, so what better way to interfere with your electronics than more energy?"

"That makes sense," Jesse said.

"He loves you so much, he is letting you know he is around by setting off the alarm clock."

The animals tell me that they do the best they can to let us know they are around us. They will utilize the resources that are around you. Your pet needs energy to manipulate objects and send signs. You can supply them with a form of spiritual fuel, which may allow them to send more signs.

Spiritual fuel consists of loving thoughts, prayers and happy memories. Imagine you are topping off their fuel supply with this powerful energy. Over time, you may begin to sense their subtle energy or start dreaming about your pet.

So Many Signs!

Other signs from the afterlife include seeing butterflies, ladybugs or dragonflies when your pet's spirit is near. Pets will also send feathers or coins to let you know they are with you. Some get really creative, and you'll hear their name on the radio or see it posted on a billboard. Some pets will even move objects around.

A deceased dog named Lefty told me he opened the cabinet where his dad, Michael, kept the dog treats. Michael laughed out loud, saying he thought he was going crazy. He would wake up in the morning, and the cabinet door would be opened. Now he loves seeing the door opened, as he knows Lefty stopped by to show his love.

Imagine how difficult it would be to move an object without a physical body. That reminds me of the movie *Ghost* with Patrick Swayze. He portrayed a character named Sam who is unexpectedly murdered. Sam had to learn how to manipulate objects after he died. He had to practice for a long time just to learn how to kick a can and move a penny without a body.

Even if you don't feel your pet around you, it doesn't mean they are gone. They are never more than a thought away and anxiously await your loving thoughts and happy memories.

Monkey the Cat

A client named Samantha contacted me for a session after her fifteen-year-old cat, Monkey, crossed over to the Other Side. The gray cat provided detailed messages about how he visited his mom in her dreams to let her know he was okay. He also showed me a frame with red hearts on it and a baby duck.

"Do you understand those references?" I asked.

"I think so." Samantha's voice was barely audible. "Everyone dreams about their pets. Why can't I feel him? I miss him so much. It's just not the same without him."

I explained to Samantha that not everyone dreams about their departed pets. Some clients tell me they would do anything to have a vivid dream about their deceased pet.

"Will you please tell my boy that I want to feel him next to me? Tell him I can't live without him, please," she begged. Samantha was sad because she wasn't receiving the type of message she wanted.

Several days later, Samantha listened to the recording of the session and realized that Monkey had shared several detailed messages that only he could know. His picture was in a *frame with red hearts* next to her bed. His favorite toy was a *little duck*. Monkey shared those specific messages so Samantha would know he was around and still a part of her life.

79

The Signs Are All Around Us

A client named Marie had a session with her deceased cat, named Pete. Before the session started, Pete asked me to talk about the lamp next to the bed and to say, "Goodnight." I asked Marie why Pete would mention the word "goodnight" and talk about a lamp. She said that after Pete died, she would wake up in the middle of the night sensing him on her bed. Each time that happened, the light on her nightstand would flicker. She said Pete's favorite time of day was at night when they would cuddle together. He always slept on the side of the bed next to the lamp, and every time she turned the light off at night, she would say goodnight to Pete and tell him how much she loved him.

During another session with a client named Greg, his deceased dog, named Jake, kept showing me a dog door. I saw the flap of the door opening and closing repeatedly with a strange clicking sound. Greg smiled through the phone as he told me that after Jake crossed over, the flap of the dog door had been opening and closing by itself. He said it made a unique clicking sound as the magnetic ends reattached. Greg thought he was going crazy, and it made him question his sanity. He was thrilled and relieved to hear that Jake was still around the house and making his presence known.

In each of these stories, you can see that our pets send us signs to let us know they are near. Most of the time they will do something they used to do when they were alive. If you haven't sensed your pet's presence or noticed any unusual activity, try not to be disheartened. It is not an indication that they don't love you or are no longer around you. Some pets are just more determined than others to get our attention. I've had some pets that send many signs of their presence and others that don't. When I check in with them, they tell me it is merely a matter of character or personal style and not due to any lack of love.

A deceased Great Dane named Cooper told me about a picture and a loud banging noise during a session one day. His mom, Teri, wasn't sure what the message meant and said she would give it some thought. After the session, she told me that she had a painting of Cooper leaning against the wall as she was deciding where to hang it in the house. The painting suddenly fell over by itself and made a loud noise as it hit the ground. Cooper was letting his mom know he was still around her and approved of the painting.

Cooper

Cooper would also leave a very special calling card whenever he visited Teri, exactly eleven cents. Cooper crossed over on May 11, and from then on, Teri would find the eleven cents everywhere she went. It was never two nickels and a penny; it was always a dime and a penny. She would find the eleven cents in the elevator, the driveway, the doctor's office; it was Cooper's way of saying, "Hi, Mom! I'm here with you!"

81

Animals Can Feel Our Emotions

When we are struggling with a loss, our pets can feel our emotions just as they did when they were here on Earth. Working through your feelings can have a positive effect on your departed pets. When you honor your grief, it moves you forward into healing and they, in turn, receive the benefit of that healing.

After the loss of a pet, emotions can be intense. It's okay to feel sad and overwhelmed during this time of grief. These emotions will not harm your pet or hold them back from their spiritual journey. Your pet loves you and wants you to heal as soon as you can.

You may struggle with your feelings as you learn how to live without the pet you love. Be patient with yourself. The grief process can take days, weeks or months to complete. There is no time frame to follow.

I like to do little things that make me happy when I'm grieving, such as splurging on a vase of freshly cut flowers, listening to my favorite music, or taking a walk in the woods.

In time, your body, mind and spirit will be ready to move forward. Your pet will be so happy to see you shifting into a place of healing. I'll share a more in-depth look at the grieving and healing process in a later chapter.

Chapter 13:
Time Does Not Exist in the Afterlife

Love goes far beyond what you call the grave.
~ Edgar Cayce

Mystery the Cat

After her cat, Mystery, crossed over, Carol contacted me to check in with her and see how she was doing. Mystery was very excited for her mom's session and could not wait to make an appearance. Two hours before her appointment, the cat appeared before me and playfully swiped her paw across my desk. I tried everything I could think of to persuade her to come back later, but she would have nothing to do with that. That crazy cat sat through two other sessions waiting for her turn. If you have ever had a little brother or sister who would stand in front of the television while you were trying to watch it, then you can relate.

Linear Time Is Non-Existent

Departed human souls get just as anxious for their session to start. One morning I got up around 6:30 a.m. to make coffee, and as I walked past my family room, I stopped dead in my tracks when I saw an old man sitting in my recliner. I lived alone, so you can imagine how startled I was. He was a full-bodied manifestation. I stood there for a moment, blinking my eyes, trying to decide if I needed to grab my shotgun. Then I realized he was a spirit person, because I could see right through him.

"Who are you?" I demanded.

"Robert," he said. "I'm watching the game."

With that, he went back to watching my television, which was turned off.

"Well, Robert, you are way too early, and you need to come back later."

He completely ignored me, picked up the remote and started cussing at the TV. I tried to send him away several more times, but he lingered around all day. I asked every client throughout the day if any of them had a grumpy relative named Robert, but no one claimed him until my last session.

"Oh yeah; that's my Uncle Bob!" said my 6:00 p.m. client, Steven. "We used to watch baseball together; never missed a game. He used to get really upset and yell at the TV."

"Oh yes; I know," I said, exhausted from my very vocal and unwelcome guest.

Once Uncle Bob delivered his messages, he disappeared into thin air.

Every session brings something new and unique, and I never know who will show up or what information will come through.

Chapter 14:
Who Will Greet My Pet on the Other Side?

Figuring out our gifts in life is part of our journey
to becoming enlightened human beings.
~ Allison DuBois, psychic medium

Most of us are curious to know who will greet our pet when they cross over. Will it be a departed human loved one? Or perhaps another pet will be waiting for them. In either case, we hope our animals will have a peaceful and smooth transition to the Other Side.

Most departed pets tell me they are greeted by family and loved ones, both human and animal. In some cases, Angels or Spirit Guides greet them, and there is always a joyous celebration.

When a client named Lynne had to say goodbye to her horse, Persia, I saw the energy of a gray mare coming through in my office. Lynne said that the gray mare was Persia's birth mother who crossed over several years earlier. It was a beautiful sight to behold seeing the two of them together in spirit.

A parrot named Nutmeg told me she was greeted by a departed grandmother. Angela told me she worried that no one would be there to greet Nutmeg, so she asked her departed grandmother to be there for her. Even though they didn't know each other in life, their love for Angela brought Nutmeg and her grandmother together on the Other Side.

Who Greets Strays or Shelter Animals?

When a stray animal crosses over, there is always a welcoming soul waiting to greet them. The same is true for shelter animals or those who don't have a loving home.

Angels, Spirit Guides or other departed animals will be the first ones to welcome them when they cross over. As far as I can tell, there are no animals floating around in the cosmos without a loving guide by their side.

As Their Final Days Approach

It sounds so simple, but thinking positive thoughts can help make things a little easier as your pet's final days approach. Tell them how loved and special they are, or talk about a favorite memory you have with them. Think of them as being happy, healthy and whole. Ask a departed loved one, human or animal, to be there to greet them when they cross over.

Your pet loves you so much, they will want to stay with you as long as they can. Be proactive about managing their pain or discomfort. Try not to keep them here any longer than necessary. Provide them with plenty of loving support and calm energy so they can make the transition out of their body peacefully.

It is very comforting to know that our loved ones will greet our pets when they die, but what will happen when we cross over? Will our animals be there to greet us?

Chapter 15:
Will My Animals Be There to Greet Me?

No heaven will not ever Heaven be.
Unless my cats are there to welcome me.
~ Anonymous

Have no fear; your pets will be near! You may have heard about the Rainbow Bridge, a mystical place where all of the departed animals you have known in your lifetime await you in a beautiful meadow. Even though the Rainbow Bridge is a fictional place, there are similarities to the Other Side. Our pets are definitely waiting for us when we cross over, and there is a joyous celebration when we arrive.

The animals tell me there is a small part of our soul that remains on the Other Side when we are here on Earth. When we cross over, we are finally reconnected to that small portion and we become whole again, or energetically complete. That's why you may have heard the Other Side referred to as *going home*. We go back to where we were created before this incarnation. Back to our creator, our divine place of origin.

A deceased cat named Peena told me that her mom Diane's soul visited her in a castle on the Other Side even though Diane was alive and well. Peena showed me the beautiful castle and described flowers and all the ornate decorations inside. Diane confirmed that she had an incredibly vivid dream-like, out-of-body experience where she visited Peena in a similar castle.

Peena

After the session, Peena left the image of this magical meeting place in the condensation on Diane's bathroom mirror. Diane sent a photo of the mirror to me, and I was shocked at how much it looked like the castle Peena showed me during the session.

One day we will all know exactly what it is like to go back home again, back to our divine place of origin surrounded by all the animals we have loved.

Chapter 16:
When Accidents Happen

*Our animal friends' non-reactive and forgiving natures can teach us
positive spiritual lessons on a daily basis.*
~ Eckhart Tolle

"I killed my dog!" came the tearful sobs over the phone. A client named Marlene accidentally closed the car door on her Chihuahua, named Princess. The little dog did not survive and died in her arms.

There are few things as devastating as losing a pet by an accident caused by our own actions. The guilt can be unbearable and cause us to alter our life so we will never feel that pain again. I've had clients tell me they will never get another pet again after an unfortunate accident takes the life of their pet. Others may punish themselves for long periods of time and carry the burden of guilt for decades.

Does Our Pet Forgive Us?

Most of the time, animals talk about happier memories and won't mention anything about the accident that took their life. They often can't or won't recall what happened to them at the moment of death. It seems as though they have little or no memory of most traumatic events.

This memory loss is similar to what humans experience during a traumatic episode. For example, people who have been in a serious accident commonly state that they have no memory of the accident. They can remember what they were doing just before the moment of impact, but not the event itself.

Animals have told me that they were here one moment and out of their body the next. They may show me the image of a car, a predator or whatever the object was that ended of their life, but they don't show it as it was happening. Their experience can be very different from what their human thought they endured.

Although animals don't want to die, they are far more accepting of their death than we are. They tell me, "My body failed" or "I left my body." Not a single pet has said that their human killed them.

When I communicated with Princess, she never mentioned the accident or anything involving the car door. Her energy was light and bright, and she shared many detailed messages with us. The horrible accident that took her life was not a part of her memory.

Tracy contacted me to check in with her deceased cat, Big Boy. She was devastated because she accidentally backed over him with her car. Big Boy survived the accident with a broken leg, but soon afterward he developed complications and died.

During the session, Big Boy spoke only about his love for Tracy and how she was his joy and treasure in life. He showed me that had he survived, there would have been worse consequences that he would have had to endure.

Suddenly, he showed me the image of an amputated leg. I assumed he meant his own leg would have to be amputated. When I told Tracy what I was seeing, she burst into tears. Unbeknownst to me, Tracy had her leg amputated several months earlier after she was involved in a horrible car accident. Big Boy was not concerned with what happened to him; instead, he showed his love and concern for his mom by talking about *her serious injuries*.

Remember:

Your intention was never to harm your pet. Know that they sense the love you have for them even when accidents happen.

When the day comes for you to see your pet again, their love will be stronger than ever. Your fur-babies are forever in your heart and a part of your eternal soul.

<u>Chapter 17:</u>
When Spirit Animals Talk

If you talk to the animals they will talk with you
and you will know each other.
If you do not talk to them you will not know them,
and what you do not know you will fear.
What one fears one destroys.
~ Chief Dan George

I've heard all kinds of messages from departed animals. Sometimes it is the last thing we expect to hear. It makes each session interesting and exciting, because you never know what your pet will talk about.

After Jack crossed over, the 200-pound Mastiff was concerned about his mom's health and sent an odd message during a session one day. Jack said, "Tell her it's in the glands."

Marilyn had not been feeling well at the time of the session and had consulted with numerous specialists who could not determine what was ailing her. Following up on Jack's message, she was shocked to find out that she had breast cancer, which had spread to her lymph nodes, or *glands*.

Fortunately, she caught it in time. And with surgery and chemotherapy, Marilyn is alive and well today, thanks to her deceased dog and the message that saved her life.

Ruby

A deceased horse named Ruby told me to say, *'Rocks and gift'* during a session with her dad, Thomas. She also said that the month of *October* would have significance. Neither of us had any clue as to what the messages meant at the time.

Almost a year later, Thomas felt compelled to visit a local horse breeder, although he had no intention of getting another horse after the loss of Ruby. He was floored when they showed him a filly by the name of *Roxy's Gift*. It just so happened to be the month of October.

Journey

A deceased cat named Journey kept telling me about a loud beeping noise. His dad, Eric, told me the smoke detector had been going off for no apparent reason even though he had replaced the batteries. Journey admitted that he was messing around with the smoke detector to let his dad know he was visiting.

Journey

Nellie

A deceased dog named Nellie told me to say, "Wolfman Jack" during a session one day. It took a while for her mom and dad, Dyan and Jon, to figure out who she was referring to. After about a month, they discovered that an old friend who went by the nickname Wolfman Jack had passed away. He loved dogs, so it only made sense that he and Nellie were together on the Other Side.

Nellie

Doobie

I was preparing for a session with a deceased dog named Doobie, when I suddenly smelled the scent of a permanent marker pen. When his dad, Frank, called for his appointment, I asked if he had been writing with a permanent marker. Frank said he had been using a black marker just before our session. The pen was sitting right in front of him during the call.

If that was not enough proof that Doobie was in the room with him, the pit bull showed me an image of an angel statue. Frank confirmed that he was looking at an angel statue that sat next to Doobie's photo at that moment.

Doobie

Albert

Albert was a deceased horse who loved to watch over his mom, Melissa. During our session, the horse told me about a *big flood*, and I saw a completely messed-up house. Melissa confirmed that the pipes in her house broke and flooded her basement.

Lady

A deceased dog named Lady told me to talk about a *"special name and poop"* during her session. As it turned out, Lady's nickname was Poop-a-lina. There

97

was even a little Poop-a-lina song she sang for me. I had that darn song stuck in my head for days.

Kiva

A very dear client named Shawn contacted me to connect with his deceased cat, named Kiva. This extraordinary cat delivered many accurate and detailed messages about jobs, relationships and family over the years. During one session, Kiva delivered some very unexpected news about a baby. Shawn said he did not know anyone that was expecting a child, and we finished up the session.

Within a month, Shawn's wife informed him they were expecting, which had been an impossibility, according to the doctors. It was one of those amazing moments when little Morgan was born, and who would have known that their deceased cat, Kiva, knew about it almost a year earlier.

Our departed pets love to share funny or eventful moments like these. It's their way of letting you know they will always love you and watch over you from the Other Side.

Chapter 18:
Animals as an Eye Witness

We find animals doing things that we,
in our arrogance, used to think was "just human."
~ Jane Goodall

During my law enforcement days, I discovered that animals could share accurate details about a crime they witnessed while they were alive. But could a deceased pet share enough information from the Other Side to solve a murder?

The body of a young woman was found in Central Park in the early 1980s. Police had a solid suspect but could not obtain DNA evidence to make an arrest. During a police interrogation, the prime suspect admitted he was in Central Park walking his dog on the day the woman went missing. I obtained a photo of his dog who had since crossed over and asked her what happened on that fateful day.

The dog confirmed that her dad attacked and killed the young woman. She was able to show me specific details about the body placement and images of the victim's clothing that were never released to the public.

In another case, a man named Brian was abducted from his home where he lived with his two cats.

The case went cold when authorities were unable to locate his body.

One of his cats was able to share specific details during the session and gave me the initials ARJ. The primary suspect in the case was a man named Arnold Roberts Jr.

The cats also described what happened the day their dad was attacked in his apartment. They described the two men who were involved and left us with a cryptic message of *1515* and *TWO SPOONS*.

No one understood those messages until many years later when Brian's body was found. A farmer plowing a field in a remote area found human remains that were later identified as Brian. The farm was located at 1515 Two Spoons Road.

I've worked enough cold cases to know that departed pets can tell me exactly what happened. Animals have no agenda or ulterior motives, so they share information in an unbiased, truthful manner. Even if the authorities were unable to make an arrest, their detailed information has provided answers, closure and peace of mind to countless victims and their families.

Chapter 19:
Oh, Those Cats!

How we behave toward cats here below
determines our status in heaven.
~ Robert A. Heinlein

Who's the Smartest Animal of All?

I'm often asked which type of animal is the most intelligent. While you may think the smartest animals are dolphins, primates or pigs, my thoughts go right back to cats.

Of course, those other species are extremely intelligent; there is no denying that, but I conduct the majority of my sessions with cats, dogs and horses. I have found that if any animal is going to make a fool out of me, it will be a cat.

An ailing elderly cat named Benji was just about on Heaven's doorstep when I checked in on him. His mom, Ronnie, contacted me to see if he was ready to cross over. When I checked in on him, I could feel his body shutting down. I told Ronnie that it probably wouldn't be too much longer before he crossed over, probably just a matter of a few days.

Well, guess who rebounded after our session. Benji regained his strength and lived for several more months. I felt like a gigantic fool. *Darn those cats. They love to prove me wrong!*

I can't get too upset when that happens. I surround animals with so much loving energy during a session, it can make them feel better long after the session ends.

A ten-year-old cat named Dudley told me he just had an upset stomach after he had been vomiting for a few days. He did not give me any indication of any other health issue, and I told his mom, Julie, that he should bounce back soon. Within days he died unexpectedly from an aggressive form of lung cancer. When I checked in on him later, he told me it was simply his time to go and there was nothing his mom or the doctors could have done for him.

There are times that I get things wrong. I am human, after all, and I do make mistakes. I try to learn from those experiences and have come to realize that try as I might, I am far from perfect and not entitled to certain information.

Chapter 20:
A Curtain of Privacy

Sometimes the most evolved souls take the most challenging paths.
~ Dr. Brian Weiss, M.D., Author of "Many Lives, Many
Masters"

Even though detailed information can come through during a session, there may be times when certain messages are blocked. We all have a curtain of privacy around us, and try as I might, there are some things I'm not entitled to know.

Don't worry, your deceased pets won't reveal your bank account numbers or passwords. They won't tell me your username or your locker combination either. Heck, I've asked for the winning lotto numbers more times than I can count.

Preventing certain information from coming through encourages us to develop our intuition and helps us learn to trust our instincts. If we are given all the answers to our problems, that would be cheating, and we wouldn't be learning from this thing called *life*.

Your private moments are also kept safely behind a protective curtain. If you think of all the compromising positions your pets have seen you in during their lifetime, thankfully, they don't share with me those images either.

The most risqué message I received was from a cat named Jezebel. She blurted out, "Mom has a pink bra!" And sure enough, Elaine told me she had just purchased a pink bra.

I didn't see the bra or Elaine wearing it; I just heard the words.

Leave it to a cat. Those felines don't miss a thing. So don't worry; you have a curtain of privacy that surrounds you, and what goes on in your private life stays private.

As you read these stories, I hope you have gained a greater understanding of how our deceased pets stay connected with us from the Other Side. In the next part of this book, we will delve into more serious topics, such as euthanasia and what our animals experience during their physical death.

I will also provide a closer look at the grieving process and share steps you can take to move through your pain into healing.

While these may be difficult subjects to discuss, hearing the animal's perspective will hopefully allow you to understand their experience in a brand new light.

Part III

Part III

<u>Chapter 21:</u>
As the End Approaches

I will never judge you for helping me leave when my body failed.
It is the ultimate gift of love.
~ Divinely communicated from the Other Side, Karen Anderson

Do Pets Choose Their Time to Cross Over?

Your pet has entrusted you to manage their life through the end of their days. As that time approaches, your emotions can cloud your judgment and make it even more difficult to determine when their time is ending.

Many departed pets have told me that they chose their time to cross over. They specifically waited until their human was gone to leave their body. Pet parents are usually shocked and dismayed when they return from a vacation or a business trip to find their beloved pet has died.

They may be overwhelmed with guilt or feel they have failed the pet they love. That is not necessarily how the animals feel. Some pets will actually wander off and find a quiet place away from home as their final hour approaches.

Takoda, the Red Heeler

My dear friends Carla and Brad awoke to find their sweet boy, Takoda, had crossed over quietly in his sleep. I originally shared Takoda's story in my book *Hear All Creatures!* when he brought Carla's Spirit Guides through during her very first session back in 2005. Koda was a handsome, twelve-year-old red heeler who was so smart, he performed just about any task asked of him and understood actual words and sentences. When he crossed over unexpectedly of heart failure, Carla and Brad were devastated and anxious to hear from their beloved boy. They felt they didn't get a chance to say goodbye, as he died while they slept.

Koda came through as happy as ever with love and excitement for his mom and dad. He told us it was the perfect time for him to leave; he said his transition out of his body was smooth as silk. He told us he was now with their other two dogs, Monty and Piper, who also crossed over earlier that year.

Just as we were finishing up, Carla asked Koda if he had a message for Brad. Koda said, "VROOOM VROOOM!"

"He's saying VROOOM VROOOM; does that make sense to you?" I asked.

Carla and Brad were elated and knew exactly what it meant. Whenever they asked, "Koda, what does the car say?" Koda would say the words, "VROOOM VROOOM."

Obviously, Koda was doing just fine and was ready to leave his body. Carla and Brad had a beautiful ceremony after burying Koda beneath one of their favorite trees.

Of all the ways for our pets to leave us, crossing over quietly in their sleep is just about as good as it gets. There is no stressful vet visit or waiting for the doctor to arrive. I have never had a pet that died quietly in their sleep. I've always had to help them cross over. I still have quite a few critters here on the farm, so maybe one of these days that will happen.

I often hear about ill or elderly cats or dogs disappearing, even if they never left the yard before. Pet parents are left wondering what happened to their beloved animal, thinking they somehow failed them.

Knowing what happened as your pet crossed over can bring forth a feeling of peace and acceptance for the pet you lost.

Pets Distance Themselves as They Prepare to Leave

Often, we fear that our animals will get lost on the Other Side if we weren't there with them when they crossed over. Some pets want us to be with them, and others prefer to die alone. It's always best to check in and find out what your pet wants during their final moments.

You may notice your pet acting strangely by distancing themselves from you. This may be an indication that they are preparing to cross over.

Some pets feel vulnerable when their body begins to slow down. They don't necessarily want the other resident animals to see them in their weakened state. Allow them to find a quiet and calm place to rest and take refuge.

In the wild, an animal will often distance themselves from their herd or pack when they are in their final days. Their instincts drive them to do this. The weak, ill or injured animals can lure predators in and potentially put the rest of the herd or pack at risk. Some animals will be driven out because they pose a risk to the remainder of the group.

They will go off by themselves and soon succumb to their illness, injury or predation. It is a survival instinct to keep the rest of the herd or pack safe.

The Nature of Animals Is to Seek a Quiet Place for Their Final Moments

It is a human concept that we must gather around the dying, hovering and tending to their every need. If your pet prefers to be alone, remember this is not a personal statement about you or an indication that they don't love you;

it's just the nature of animals. They are merely following their strong instincts and acting in accordance with what Mother Nature intended.

Allow your pet to maintain a sense of dignity as they prepare to leave this Earth.

How to Help Your Pet Prepare to Leave

Make your pet as comfortable as possible in their final days. Watch their body language and physical clues to determine their needs. Tell them out loud how much you love them and how grateful you are for the life you shared together.

Tips to help your pet prepare to cross over:

- Stay emotionally calm, as strong feelings can make the final moments more difficult for your pet.
- Keep them quiet and isolated from noise, other animals and young children.
- Try not to hover or overstimulate with affection.
- Let them isolate themselves if they choose.
- Think loving thoughts and happy memories.
- Invite your departed loved ones to greet them when they cross over.
- Envision them as being released from a body that has failed them.
- Imagine them going to a beautiful place filled with warmth, comfort and love.
- Provide them with a blanket, towel or shirt that you have recently used so they have your scent with them, particularly at the veterinarian's office.
- Talk soothingly, use a soft voice, and find peace in your heart to let them go.

- Tell them you will miss them so much, but you understand it is their time to leave.

If you feel your pet is nearing the end of their days, do your best to honor their needs. Your calm, loving energy will help them make a smooth transition out of their body.

Chapter 22:
Euthanasia:
The Impossible Decision

The day you took your last breath was the day my world went dark.
~ Lynda Cheldelin Fell

When your pet's final days arrive, the daunting decision of euthanasia looms overhead like a dark cloud. Anyone who has been faced with this impossible decision knows firsthand how difficult and confusing this time can be.

The final days are torturous, like an emotional roller coaster ride. There are good days when things seem to be improving; then there are bad days when you question your selfishness for keeping your pet alive.

Sometimes animals will miraculously recover and start acting like themselves again, and just when you think they have turned the corner into healing, the inevitable happens, and they go into a downward spiral.

This usually happens late at night, on a weekend, or on a holiday, the most inopportune time. There is no good time for your pet's days to run out. It brings us to the decision none of us ever want to make, the impossible decision to end our beloved pet's life.

Is it Right to End Their Life?

We know the day will eventually come when we have to say goodbye. Many of us secretly hope that our pet will pass away peacefully in their sleep and we won't have to go through with this unimaginable deed. We spend our lives taking care of them, and the last thing we want to do is end their life.

Some say that it's not right to take a life. Others feel that it is cruel to allow them to suffer when we can humanely end their pain. Regardless of our opinions, the love we feel for our pets is universal and remains our common bond. The power of love we feel for our pets unites us.

Many clients report that they had no idea their pet was ill. They say they were fine one moment and in a health crisis the next. While that may be your initial thought, once you start looking back at their behavior, there are often telltale signs that we dismissed or overlooked.

Dismissing Strange Behavior

It happens to many of us, and I am no exception. I've brushed off strange behaviors or issues with my pets, thinking it was nothing serious.

Then when that pet died, I carried that burden of guilt. You might think that I have it easy because I can communicate with my pets, but that's not always the case. While I can ask how they are doing and determine their level of pain, I still have to utilize common sense and learn from past experiences.

Over the years, I've learned to pay attention to the details and subtle clues, and I do my best to stay in front of the curve with any known health issues. It's still not foolproof, and things still get by me, but I no longer disregard odd behaviors.

Is Euthanasia Less Stressful?

Some people believe they should let their pet die on their own. That is the way it would happen in the wild if we weren't in the picture. While that may be true, pets who pass on their own will often tell me that it was a struggle, there was a significant level of suffering, or they were in pain before they died.

Because of that, I am an advocate for euthanizing whenever possible. The animals tell me there is far less emotional and physical trauma when they are euthanized. By staying calm, you can help your pet move through their final moments more peacefully. Ultimately, deciding whether or not to euthanize your pet is a personal choice, and you should do what feels right in your heart. No matter what you decide, there is a lot of guilt associated with the end of your pet's life.

When Is the Right Time to Euthanize?

Some of us feel guilty about choosing to euthanize our pet instead of paying for an expensive procedure. We struggle with the decision about when to euthanize and wonder if our pet will be upset with us or if they will ever forgive us for taking their life.

We worry that they are suffering or in pain. We may ask ourselves the same questions over and over. Was it the right time? Did I wait too long? Or did I end their life too soon? I'll talk about that actual moment of death in a later chapter, but now let's explore how to know when it is the right time to say goodbye.

A Personal Decision Only You Can Make

Finding the right time to euthanize your pet is a personal decision between you, your veterinarian and your pet. I will not tell you when to euthanize, but

I can help you determine how your pet feels, their pain or discomfort levels, and if they are ready to leave their body.

Some animals are extremely tolerant of their health issues and tell me they are doing just fine. Others have begged me to tell their human to help them leave their body. You know your animal better than anyone, so it's always best that you go with your instincts and trust your intuition.

If you are still confused about what to do, consider stepping outside of your feelings and think about what is best for your pet. What decision would prevent them from having to endure unnecessary pain?

As a pet parent, try to act on their behalf and decide based on what is best for your pet.

Consider your attitudes about a terminal illness or the dying process before your pet reaches that point. Think of death as a release, not an end, but a beginning to a new spiritual afterlife.

<u>Chapter 23:</u>
The Sting of Death

Goodbyes are not forever.
Goodbyes are not the end.
They simply mean I'll miss you until we meet again!
~ Author Unknown

Watching your pet during the moment of euthanasia can be a difficult sight to behold. I've had to do it many times, and it never gets any easier. The injection can sting as it enters their bloodstream, and your pet may cry out in discomfort.

Some veterinarians will give them a sedative to calm them, but that may slow down their circulatory system. It may take longer for the lethal drug to move through their system.

Animals rarely mention the struggle you may see before they cross over. Most of the time that struggle is their natural reflexes as the heart stops. They are usually so exhilarated to be out of their bodies that any signs of distress that you witness are not a part of their experience.

If you feel guilty about having to euthanize your pet, here are a few things to consider. When you come from a place of love in your heart, when your intention is to do the right thing for your pet, they sense this and do not hold you responsible.

Think about this scenario for just a moment. Every day of your pet's life, you set out to care for them and love them with all your heart. You fed them, medicated them, and probably changed your schedule around to accommodate their needs.

Your pets know how much you love them, and they sense that you have only the best intentions when you are helping them leave their body.

It would be an entirely different story if every day you set out to cause your animal nothing but pain and misery. If your intention was to do them harm, then the animals sense that. Since that is not the case, you can rest assured knowing that your good intentions come through loud and clear to your pet.

Fortunately, the last few moments on this Earth don't seem imperative to the animals. Rarely do they describe the brink of death as anything other than exhilarating.

The best thing you can do to help your pet in their last moments is to stay calm and surround them with loving thoughts.

Chapter 24:
Cremation or Burial?

How lucky I am to have something
that makes saying goodbye so hard.
~ Winnie the Pooh

What Our Pets Want

What is the right thing to do with our animal's remains? Do we opt for cremation and put their urn on a shelf in our living room? Do we leave them at the veterinary office to be disposed of in a mass grave? What about backyard burials or spreading ashes in a favorite location? While this is a difficult subject to discuss, it is a reality we must face when we say goodbye to a dear and devoted friend.

Most decisions are made under stressful situations or when our animals become gravely ill. I've heard a lot of interesting stories about what people do with their animals' remains, from taxidermy to burials and just about everything in between. The responses from the animals are always insightful and offer a new point of view.

Truffles

Perri already made the decision of what to do with the remains of her beloved Yorkshire Terrier when the day came to say goodbye. As her aging dog, Truffles, was approaching the end of her physical life, the thought of being without her was overwhelming. She couldn't bear to think about going forward in life without seeing her beloved companion, so she arranged to have Truffles preserved through cryopreservation. This freeze-drying method of preservation offers a unique alternative to cremation or burial.

Truffles

Truffles was excited about her life-like image and said she felt "very loved and very special" when the process was complete.

"That's me!" she said with a big smile.

The results were impressive, and it gave Perri the peace of mind to see her sweet girl sitting life-like on her pink pillow. This was certainly the exception to what most people decide to do with their animal's remains, but here are a few more cases that come to mind.

Cremation

When Bill and Andrea asked me to connect with their deceased cat, named Max, he showed me a wooden box with his name etched on it.

"We have that wooden box sitting right here next to the fireplace." They were thrilled that Max knew about it. "It gives us a sense of peace knowing his remains are near us. It makes us feel like he is still here, still with us."

Melissa scheduled a session to connect with her two deceased cats, Lilly and Penny. When I opened up to Lilly's energy, she kept showing me her silky black fur. "Talk about the fur," she said. I thought perhaps Lilly was just a very silky kitty and wanted to show Melissa how vibrant she looked on the Other Side.

When I checked in with Penny, she told me to say, "I'm right next to her heart," and kept showing me the shape of a Valentine's heart.

Melissa explained how much those messages meant to her, because after each cat had passed away, she placed a portion of their ashes and fur in a heart-shaped locket, and she wore it every day. Both cats were happy that their mom thought about them every day as she wore the locket. They could feel the love Melissa had for them, and that's what made them happy.

How Pets Feel About Burial

Most animals do not feel connected to their remains after they cross over. They are usually very excited for their new afterlife journey to start. Very few pets mention what happened to their remains.

Sandra was devastated when her husband left their deceased dog, Sammy, at the veterinary office to be disposed of in a mass grave while she was away on business.

Ever since he died, she was worried that Sammy was lost in the afterlife and unable to find his way. Not so, reported Sammy. He was not the least bit concerned about what happened to his body.

"I'm no longer there," he said, as he proceeded to show me images of a backyard with a pool and covered patio. "Tell her I'm right here," he said.

Sandra was so relieved, as Sammy used to love to float on a raft in their backyard pool oasis.

Do What Makes You Happy

The majority of pets I communicate with are not attached to their physical remains after death. They love when we think about them, so do whatever feels right to you. If your pet disappeared or you don't have their remains, conducting a ceremony, prayer, lighting a candle, or just remembering them with love will suffice.

Your pet will feel honored and special when you remember them as they were in life — happy, healthy and whole. Ultimately, they are okay with whatever makes you happy.

Do Animals Have a Soul?

I've heard some theories that animals don't have souls or that when they die, they go into a group consciousness and don't keep their individual character traits. I have not found that to be the case.

Each of the animals I connect with maintain their unique personality. As an animal's soul progresses on the Other Side, they can choose to move into a collective consciousness. Merging with this type of soul group is rejuvenating for all, and yet they still stay connected to the humans they love.

Chapter 25:
The Journey Through Grief

*Grief is not meant to be the soul's final destination; rather a resting
place for the heart as we emerge onto the path of healing.*
~ Divinely communicated from the Other Side, Karen Anderson

Coping with the loss of a pet you love is one of life's most difficult challenges. Often, the pain can feel overwhelming. You may experience all kinds of unexpected emotions, from denial, shock or anger to guilt, disbelief and profound sadness.

The pain of grief can also disrupt your physical health, making it difficult to eat, sleep or even think clearly. These are common reactions when suffering from a significant loss.

Your pets love you so much they want you to heal as soon as you can. They watch over you, diligently waiting by your side as you move through the stages of grief.

As difficult as it is to suffer a loss, there are healthy ways to cope with the pain. But before we explore those steps, we need to take a closer look at what grief is and is not.

Grief is defined as a normal and natural reaction to a significant loss of any kind. There are many different triggers, such as the loss of a job or a relationship, but the loss of a pet or loved one is one of the most profound losses we experience.

What Grief Is Not

Grief is not a disease or an illness. It is not a pathological condition or a personality disorder. ***Grief is not depression***, rather depression may be brought about by our grief. It is not a sign of weakness or a reflection of poor character. It is not easy to recover from a significant loss.

Common Symptoms of Grief

While a loss affects people in different ways, keep in mind that almost anything that you experience in the early stages of grief is normal.

Shock, disbelief, sadness, anger and guilt are some of the most common symptoms of grief. You may also have feelings of despair, emptiness or intense loneliness.

You may also cry a lot or feel emotionally unstable. Others may not be able to cry. Crying is a normal response to sadness, but it's not the only one. Those who don't cry may feel the pain just as deeply as those who do cry. They may simply have other ways of showing it.

Physical Symptoms

We often think of grief as a strictly emotional process, but grief often involves physical problems, including fatigue, nausea, lowered immunity, weight loss or weight gain, aches and pains, and insomnia.

Broken Heart Syndrome

Experiencing extreme physical pain from a loss is a sign of deep love, severe stress, and may be a condition known as the *Broken Heart Syndrome*.

Women are more susceptible to this condition and should seek help at the first sign of physical pain. For more information about *Broken Heart Syndrome*, go to www.heart.org.

Chapter 26:
After a Pet Dies

Ever has it been that love knows not its own depth
until the hour of separation.
~ Kahlil Gibran

After the loss of a pet, many people struggle with what to say to the person suffering from a loss. It's not easy to talk to someone about losing their pet.

We don't want to upset them or make them uncomfortable, so many times we say nothing. When we do say something, the words can come out all wrong.

Here are a few things to **avoid saying** when someone has suffered a loss:

- **Now they are in a better place.** This implies they were in a horrible place with us.
- **At least they aren't in pain anymore.** This implies we allowed them to suffer.
- **You can always adopt another pet.** This means our pet was disposable. We don't want another pet. We want our pet.
- **It is part of God's plan.** This implies that God's plan is to cause us extreme pain.
- **At least you have your other pets to love.** I don't want my other pets. I want this pet.

- **It is time to get on with your life.** I'm not ready to move on. Now I feel even worse.
- **I know how much you loved him/her.** No, you don't how much love I had for this pet.
- **I know how you feel.** You don't know how my pain feels.
- **They lived a long happy life with you. You should be happy about that.** No, I'm actually very sad that they are gone. Losing a pet I love after so many years hurts.
- **With as many pets as you have, you should be used to this by now.** No, I'll never get used to the pain. Each loss brings about a new feeling of pain.

Other Statements to Avoid

- **Avoid comparing your pain.** For example, "I just lost my cat, and I know how you feel." No, you don't know how I feel. My feelings are my own.
- **Avoid telling gruesome stories of other pet's deaths.** Such as, "My sister just ran over her dog; it was horrible."
- **Avoid trying to cheer them up.** They may not be ready.
- **Avoid asking if that person is okay.** They are not okay; they are in the depths of despair.

When someone you know has suffered the loss of a pet, try to be sensitive to their fragile emotions. Perhaps you can remember how you felt after you suffered a loss. Kindness goes a long way as you will see in the next chapter.

<u>Chapter 27</u>:
How to Help
After a Loss

Every positive thought propels you in the right direction.
~ Author Unknown

A fter a loss, many times we just want our loss to be acknowledged. We don't want to be fixed; we want our feelings to be heard. It helps us work through our feelings when we can share how deeply we loved the pet we lost.

Here are a few examples of what **you can say** when someone has suffered a loss:

Acknowledge their loss:
- "I'm so sorry to hear that (say their name) has passed away. I can't imagine how difficult this must be for you."
- "I'm sorry you are going through this difficult time."
- "I'm here for you."
- "If I can do anything at all, just let me know."
- "If you want to talk, I'm here."

More Ways to Help

Check in with them in the days, weeks and months after a loss. It only takes a second, but it means a lot to that person.

- Sometimes just being there with them not saying a word is helpful.
- Some people want to be alone. So text or reach out to let them know you care.
- Bring them flowers, send them a card, or make a donation in memory of their pet.

Imagine you are topping off that person's heart with love. Quietly in your mind, fill them up with positive thoughts. Every loving word or kind thought will be appreciated.

Chapter 28:
How to Heal

Healing is an art. It takes time, it takes practice. It takes love.
~ Maza Dohta

W̲e must each find our way through the shroud of grief into healing. The pain of grief can often cause you to withdraw from others and retreat into a world of pain. Some of us need this time to be alone, and we find peace in our solitude. We feel better by keeping to ourselves and working our way through our grief privately.

Others may prefer the companionship of others and feel better when surrounded by family or friends. Do whatever feels right to you. If you seek the companionship of others, give yourself permission to focus on other topics other than your loss.

Find Support After a Loss

Most of us will have a network of loved ones or coworkers who want to be supportive after a loss. It is the perfect time to lean on the people who care about you, even if you take pride in being strong and self-sufficient. Reach out to friends and family members, or find a grief support group.

Draw Comfort From Your Faith or Spiritual Beliefs

If you follow a religious tradition, embrace the comfort that mourning rituals can provide. Spiritual activities that are meaningful to you, such as praying, meditating or going to church, can offer solace.

If you're questioning your faith in the wake of the loss, talk to a clergy member or others in your religious community for guidance.

Support From Others Can Help You Heal

Join a support group or find a grief counselor who can help you work through your emotions. They can help get you on the path to healing. It is so important to take care of yourself and ask for assistance if you need it. Your departed pets love you so much, and they want to you to heal as soon as you can.

Suicide

In a few rare cases, I have had clients tell me they wanted to end their lives as they no longer wanted to live without their beloved pet. Fortunately, with my law enforcement background, I was trained to handle suicidal situations and encouraged each of them to seek counseling and recover from their grief.

Remember, your pets love you more than anyone else in the world, and they want you to live out the rest of your life with joy and happiness in your heart. Someday, when it is our time to cross over, we will be reunited with our departed loved ones, and our bonds of love will be stronger than ever.

Resources:

For more information, go to www.helpguide.org.

Chapter 29:
Reincarnation

You were born and died many times.
You are the soul who lived all of your lives.
~ *"The Afterlife of Billy Fingers," a true story by Annie Kagan*

Before I became a psychic, the topic of reincarnation intrigued me. I was fascinated by the idea. I was fairly confident that we do come back and experience another lifetime or two. Now, after two decades of validations, I'm entirely convinced that animals reincarnate, sometimes more than once in a lifetime.

I've witnessed dozens of cases with verified facts of animals reincarnating and returning to their beloved people. While they are all incredibly amazing stories, one story about reincarnation stands out among all the others.

Captain

Frank contacted me when he lost his five-year-old pit bull from a genetic illness. Frank was devastated by this unexpected loss and reached out to me in the hopes of reconnecting with his dog, Captain.

Captain

At first, Frank was very skeptical and thought reincarnation was "all a bunch of hogwash," as he later told me. But the sudden loss of Captain led him to investigate further.

Frank said he Googled many psychics, but eventually he was drawn to my website. I believe Captain steered Frank in my direction.

As soon as Frank asked Captain if he would return to him, I immediately started to receive vivid images and messages.

Captain told me that Frank would find him on a Wednesday and that a human female would be involved. Captain also mentioned the letter "T" as having significance, and there was a reference to something "big."

Captain said there would be a very visible sign and kept mentioning the letter "C." Armed with those messages, Frank set out with renewed hope that he would once again have Captain back in his life.

About three months later, I received an email from Frank with a picture of a tiny pit bull puppy. Frank wanted to know if this was his "Little C," which is what he used to call Captain.

As I opened the photo, I heard Captain say, "It is me!" And I could feel his excitement wash over me. I told Frank, "Little C is here!"

The puppy (Cash) had the letter 'C' on his head.

All the Clues Lined Up

Frank said everything lined up when he was looking for his new puppy. He found him on a Wednesday, a woman named Toni had the puppies, and there was the letter 'C' on the puppy's head.

Frank named the puppy Cash to honor Captain. When I saw the photo of this tiny, little puppy, I could not believe my eyes. On his head in plain sight was the letter 'C.' Now that's a clear sign!

The only message that didn't fit at the time was Captain's reference to something "big." It would be several years later when that message would finally make sense. In a recent visit to the veterinary office, Cash weighed in at a whopping 133 pounds. Now that's big!

As I was writing this chapter, I asked Frank what this experience was like for him. He said, "It was shocking. I couldn't believe it. Miracles do happen. I'm a believer now, all thanks to you, Karen."

I can't take all the credit; it was Captain who made it all happen. It was a group effort, and it was the right time for both of them to reunite. This case was fascinating, especially with the letter 'C' on the puppy's head. Reuniting Frank and Captain was a moment I will never forget.

Cash is now full grown and so handsome!

No Rule Books About Reincarnation

There are many different beliefs and viewpoints about reincarnation. Some are similar to my experiences with the animals, and other perspectives are way out in the cosmos. I can only speak from my personal experiences and share what I have learned over the years and from the animals themselves.

First of all, there is no rule book with checklists and requirements on whether or not your pet will reincarnate. At least I've yet to find such a book.

However, there is a Universal Law that governs each animal's soul and their future incarnations. Each embodiment has a unique and meaningful purpose, and an animal's soul may reincarnate once, multiple times or never.

This Universal Law is often referred to as a soul contract, Akashic record or life book. These contracts are not written in stone; rather they serve as a guide, or navigational tool, and as situations shift, so can the agreements.

I have learned that we are each a part of a soul group consisting of animals, humans and Spirit Guides. Within our soul group, we have an understanding with the other souls to assist each other to learn and grow while we are in physical form.

That understanding or agreement includes future incarnations. Before each of our physical lives on Earth, we select the lessons we will learn and the other people and animals who will provide us with the optimum opportunity for accomplishing those lessons.

Lessons may be about learning patience or tolerance if you have an especially challenging pet. Other lessons include compassion, forgiveness and courage. Each pet brings us a new lesson, and usually the most challenging pet provides us with our greatest life lesson.

Our agreements with our pets can shift if situations change. For instance, if you and your pet, such as a horse, have an agreement to share another lifetime together, then when the right situation presents itself, the pet's soul can reincarnate.

However, if the situation changes, such as if you move from a farm to an apartment, your agreement with your horse will shift. Since you can't have a horse in an apartment, the horse can choose to return as a smaller pet, such as a bird, cat or small dog.

Do All Animals Reincarnate?

In my experience, I have found that not all animals reincarnate. Some animals tell me they have completed their mission with us, and there is no need for them to return. Other times I hear that the animals are excited and ready to return when the time is right.

Playing Favorites

Have you ever wondered why you grieved more for one pet than another? We love them all, but there seems to be that one animal that is unmistakably more special than the rest. We try hard not to play favorites, but sometimes there is no denying the fact that we have a stronger bond with that one special pet.

The main reason for this lies in the number of times you have shared a past life with that particular pet. Your souls have been together hundreds of times, if not more. It only makes sense that on a soul level, the two of you will bond more closely than you will with a pet you have not shared a past life with before.

Our past-life experiences with our pets are cumulative, and we carry that energetic memory forward into the next lifetime. Therefore, the pet that has been with you through hundreds of incarnations will be the one that has the strongest effect on you.

So relax; you're not really playing favorites. You're just experiencing the joys of multiple incarnations with that pet.

Methods of Reincarnation

There are many different ways an animal can reincarnate. In my sessions, I have encountered three primary methods: the Newborn Method, the Walk-In Method and the Soul-Sharing Method. Keep in mind that each animal is unique, and the circumstances around their reincarnation will be as individual as they are.

Newborn Method

The most common type of reincarnation is known as the Newborn Method. It encompasses a complete circle of life. With this approach, a pet will pass away and spend quite a bit of time on the Other Side. There are no set limits, but I have noticed a pattern of about three to five years or more.

When the right opportunity presents itself, the animal will begin the search for a new body. In most cases, the pet that died will move into the body at conception or just after.

I've also had cases where the pet that died told me that it moved into the newly born body right about the time they open their eyes. If you are familiar with newborns, there is a period where they don't show much personality. They eat, sleep and nurse, but they all act the same. Suddenly, their unique personality traits will surface, and some pets tell me that corresponds to the time they move into that soul.

Animals that reincarnate through this method tend to live a normal lifespan, as they have had plenty of time to rest and rejuvenate on the Other Side.

Keep in mind the reincarnated soul will not be a clone of your prior pet. An essence of the old and new pet will form. Most of the time, a deceased pet will delay reincarnating until their human has moved through their grief and into healing.

A Walk-In

A Walk-In occurs when an animal dies and then immediately returns and walks into a new body. There is only a short time spent on the Other Side. The lifetime of a Walk-In may be shorter but very meaningful. By spending time on the Other Side after physical death, an animal rejuvenates and languishes in pure energetic love. The longer they are in that loving space of renewal, the longer their next lifetime will be.

Sadie Comes Back

When Cindy lost her cat, named Sadie, she contacted me to find out if Sadie would reincarnate. The deceased cat told us she planned to come back right away and described how she would look and where Cindy could find her.

A short time later, Cindy reported that she reunited with Sadie II and sent me several adorable pictures of her new kitten. She was thrilled to have her sweet girl back again. Sadly, within a short time, Sadie II came down with a deadly virus and died in Cindy's arms.

The first Sadie.

We had a session with Sadie II to check in on her about two months after she crossed over. During that session, she shared many loving messages, but one of them shocked Cindy to the core.

Sadie II said she was worried about Cindy smoking so much and asked if she liked the balloons she had sent her. Cindy gasped out loud and told me that the day before was her birthday, and she was really missing Sadie. While she was at work, she went outside for a cigarette break. She noticed something moving across the walkway and saw some helium birthday balloons stuck in the bushes. Sadie II said she sent the balloons and wanted to be sure her mom knew she loved her and was thinking about her on her birthday.

Sadie II

Even though Sadie II had a short life, both cats were able to be with Cindy during a very difficult time of her life. Knowing they were still connected to her, even sending birthday balloons, Cindy was able to navigate more easily through this traumatic time and into a place of healing.

Soul Sharing

Another method of reincarnation is when an animal returns as an older spirit and shares a soul with an existing animal. These lifetimes also tend to be shorter than the average lifespan, as the sharing of souls can wear the physical body down twice as fast as normal.

John contacted me several months after his Rottweiler, named Luna, died. He said a stray dog showed up at his work, and he felt an uncanny bond with the dog.

John said it was like they had known each other for years. The stray dog, he called Bronco, had many of the same habits Luna had. He described it as watching a dog with multiple personalities, and he wanted to know if he was crazy or imagining things.

I checked in with Luna, and she told me she had returned to John as a *shared soul*. She described Bronco's appearance and said she wanted to be there for her dad during a difficult time.

I shared those messages with John, and he confirmed that he had just been through a divorce and lost custody of his kids. He was depressed and lonely, and Luna saw an opportunity to return as a shared soul with the stray dog to spend more time with her dad.

John was relieved to hear he wasn't imaging things, and he was very excited that Luna had returned. Their time together lasted another two years until Bronco came down with an aggressive form of cancer. He died within a few short months of his diagnosis, but he was able to help John through a very lonely time.

Common Misconceptions About Reincarnation

Here are a few misconceptions about reincarnation:

- **An animal can only reincarnate at birth or as a newborn.** False. As I described above, there are several ways, including Walk-Ins, Soul Sharing and Newborn methods, to name a few.
- **If you try hard enough, you can make your animal reincarnate.** False. Only the pre-determined agreement decides whether the animal will return. No amount of praying, wishing or hoping will bring them back if it was not meant to be.

- **A dog can only reincarnate as a dog, and a cat can only return as a cat.** False. If it is in the highest and best interest of that soul, it can return as another type of species. Most of the time, animals return as the species they were before they died.

- **A pet must look exactly like they did in their previous life.** False. An animal will show me what their new body will look like if it has been selected. I will see size, shape and color of their new form.

- **An animal cannot reincarnate as a human, or vice versa.** False. I've had cases where an animal returned as a human. There is a significant amount of difference in a human soul vibration than that of a pet's vibration, but it can happen.

- **The gender of the pet must be the same as they were before.** False. I've seen animals return as male or female. It doesn't seem to matter to the pets as much as it does to the human.

- **Your pet will go on to live with someone else if you can't find them after they reincarnate.** False. Your pet is meant to be with you and only you.

- **When a pet reincarnates, it will be an exact clone of the pet that died.** False. Reincarnation is not cloning, and your deceased animal's soul will combine with the new soul.

- **If a pet doesn't reincarnate, it means they don't love us or we were a bad parent.** False. It wasn't intended to be. It is not a reflection of love or parenting. If it was predetermined before this lifetime, it will happen.

- **A pet can only reincarnate one time during our life.** False. I've seen it happen multiple times. Keep in mind, the subsequent lifetimes were shorter than normal.

How to Invite Pets Back

There are a few things you can do to prepare for your pet's reincarnation. As I mentioned earlier, if it isn't meant to be, it won't happen, but you can invite your departed animals to join you again if it is their highest and best interest to do so. Tell them they are welcome to return when the time is right for both of you on a spiritual level. You can do this as prayer form, quietly in your mind, or out loud as if they were there in the room with you.

It is humbling to realize that pets won't reincarnate based on our needs alone. Our pre-birth agreements and Universal Laws govern the souls destined for reincarnation.

Pets Choose to Stay on the Other Side

Departed pets tell me they are able to help us with greater ease from the Other Side than while they are here in physical form. It's one of their greatest joys to love us, watch over us, and help us live our lives to the fullest.

The most important thing to remember about reincarnation is that animals are more likely to return to us when we have moved through our grief and have completed the healing process.

One of the most valuable lessons we will learn from our pets comes from our grief and the pain of saying goodbye. It's unlikely they will return before we have completed that lesson. Take your time and work through your grief, honor your feelings, and celebrate the time you had with your pet.

Chapter 30:
One Last Story

When you see your loved ones in the Afterlife
it will be more loving than it was on Earth.
~ *"The Afterlife of Billy Fingers," a true story by Annie Kagan*

Now that we have come to the end of this book, I wanted to leave you with one final story that I feel sums up how deeply our pets love us. It is an eternal and everlasting love that knows no limits or boundaries.

Our pets love us completely when they are here on Earth and continue to be a part of our lives after they cross over. They long for us to remember them with a smile on our face and celebrate the time we shared rather than focus on a sad ending. They keep a constant vigil by our side until the day arrives for us to be together again.

At the exact moment that we leave this Earth behind, our beloved pets will be there waiting for us to come back home — back to where we came from before this incarnation.

Guru the Terrier Mix

One afternoon, I was preparing for an upcoming session with Dennis, a retired firefighter, and his deceased terrier mix, Guru. Even before Dennis called my office, Guru's energy came through loud and clear. There was also a very reluctant human female energy hovering around the little dog.

"My dad is hurting," the little black and white dog confided with me. "I'm going to help him. His heart hurts."

At the time, I just assumed that he meant his dad was hurting because Guru had recently crossed over, so I wasn't too surprised to hear this. Pets often tell me that they can feel their human's sorrow when they pass away, so I assumed that's what Guru meant.

I finished my meditation and waited for Dennis to call in for his appointment. We started the session, and Guru sent many more detailed messages, including his concern for a recent fall that Dennis had. Guru described a pretty bad break involving multiple fractures in the bones.

Dennis was stunned. "How can he see that?" he asked. "I broke my leg in two places about a month ago. Guru has been gone for three months. That's just crazy that he knows about it."

I explained to Dennis how Guru's energy is around him, and he can see what is happening to him.

"Those are powerful bonds of love between you two," I said. "I'm not surprised that he is watching over you."

What happened next floored him.

"An older human energy is coming through with Guru; it feels like a mom or grandmother energy. I hear an 'L' name as in Laura or Linda," I said. Dennis took a deep breath but didn't say a word.

"This female energy is holding Guru in her arms."

Dennis Was Not Ready to Forgive

"Are you open to hearing from this person? It feels like your mom or grandma," I asked, sensing that something was very wrong between the two of them.

Dennis hesitated and then replied, "I guess so."

Dennis described the strained relationship he had with his mom, Lorinda. In fact, she refused to let him see her in her final moments, as they had been out of touch with each other for many years.

"She hated dogs," he said. "In fact, mom wouldn't let me have a dog when I was a kid. That's weird that they would be together."

Dennis explained that his mom had a hard time showing him any affection in life. He said she was addicted to alcohol and pain medication, and from early in life, he never felt loved.

"She didn't want to waste any money on a pet. I'm pretty sure it was so she could buy more booze," he said.

I explained to Dennis that because both his mom and Guru loved him, they were connected together in his soul group on the Other Side.

"My mom didn't love me," he said bitterly. "I was a burden, an inconvenience to her. I think the only thing she loved was getting drunk."

Dennis wasn't ready to hear what I had to say next.

"She says to tell you that she is quite fond of Guru. She says the dog is helping her learn how to love. He is helping her see that she made some big mistakes in her life. "

Lorinda wasn't ready to express her love for her son, but this was a step in the right direction. She was making an effort by showing up for the session and expressing her feelings for Dennis' dog.

Some people can change their ways and see things from a different perspective once they cross over. Dennis's mom was no exception. She was learning how to open up and how to express her love for her son, all because of Guru.

A Transformation Begins

Dennis scheduled several follow-up sessions with me, and each time his mom's energy came through. I noticed how Dennis's attitude was transforming during our conversations. He laughed more, shared happy memories with Guru, and seemed genuinely interested to hear from his mom.

Dennis became a regular client, and every month or so, we would connect and catch up on what was happening in his life.

When Dennis missed an appointment, I knew right away that something was wrong. I emailed him several times but never heard back. I hoped he was just busy with his life. But about two months later, I received an unexpected card in the mail. The card was from his sister, Kristen.

"Dear Karen,

I'm reaching out to let you know that my brother, Dennis, passed away quietly in his sleep last month. He probably never let on that he suffered from a severe heart condition which weakens connective tissue around the heart. He battled this disease for many years. We thought for sure that we would lose him when his beloved dog, Guru, died two years ago. Amazingly enough, after he first communicated through your sessions, Dennis' condition stabilized.

Before he found you, Karen, Dennis was a very depressed man. He sank deeper and deeper into the depths of despair after the loss of Guru. All of that changed because of you, and that's why I'm sending you this note. Dennis looked forward to your sessions so much and found great peace of mind hearing from Guru. A total bonus was when you were able to connect with our estranged mother, whom he was finally able to forgive.

I have to admit; I did not believe in psychics, and when he told me about his sessions with you, I thought it was all a bunch of hooey. I am now a believer, and after witnessing my brother's transformation, I just want you to know what a blessing you were to him, and to all of us.

He looked forward to your sessions, and I believe it gave him a new purpose for living after he was ready to give up on life.

I would like to know if I can set up a session with you to connect with my brother and whoever else decides to come through.

Thank you for your incredible talent and giving me two more good years with my brother."

The irony looking back was that Guru told me from the very first session that his *dad's heart hurt*. I assumed that he meant emotional pain. Now I realize he was referring to Dennis' heart condition, as well as his emotional pain.

Now I look forward to my sessions with Kristen. Both Guru and Dennis' mom greeted Dennis when he crossed over. It warms my heart now that Dennis and his beloved dog are back together again.

I wrote this poem after the first session I had with Dennis. I never gave it to him in person, but I read it to him after he crossed over. His face beamed with love, and he affectionately gave me two thumbs up.

Dear Human,
It happened again today.
I nestled in right by your side
and lovingly watched over you while you slept. There isn't anywhere else that I would rather be than with you.
I nudged you gently a few times, but you barely stirred.
When you awoke, I circled joyously around your feet, smiled at you with my eyes,
then watched you gather your things and leave for work.
My loving energy surrounded you as you drove down the highway and I placed my head tenderly upon on your arm.
For a moment, you thought of me, and I felt your heart fill with sorrow.
I tried again to let you know I was right there, right by your side,
but you pushed thoughts of me away as the pain was too deep.
I wish you knew that when you feel sad, so too, do I.
When you feel joy, so too, do I.
I kept a constant vigil throughout the day
and waited patiently for you to remember me, and all the fun times we shared.
Instead, I watched helplessly as thoughts of guilt and regret overcame you, and tears filled your eyes.
Just know I will never judge you for helping me leave when my body failed.
In my mind, you gave me the ultimate gift of love.

I am alive and well in spirit and hunger for just one moment of your time when you think of me
with love and joy,
and celebrate the life we shared.
I will try again tomorrow, and the next day, and the next.
Remember dear human; our souls are connected for eternity as the bonds of love never die.

By Karen Anderson

There Is Nowhere Else Our Pets Would Rather Be

Just as in the first story with Bandit and Choo Choo, our departed pets continue to stay connected to us and are never more than a thought away. They rejoice when we are happy and watch over us in our darkest moments. It does not matter how many years go by, as time does not exist in the afterlife. Their love for us is eternal, and they patiently await the moment we will be reunited on the Other Side. As you think about your departed pets, imagine them right there with you snuggled in by your side, as there is nowhere else they would rather be.

Afterword

We've covered a lot of territory since that very first story, and I hope I have presented new and exciting points to ponder about animals in the afterlife.

Hopefully, you have a deeper sense of what happens after your pets cross over and leave their physical bodies behind. Your pets are happy, healthy and whole on the Other Side and love you more than ever. They are here to help you learn, love and grow as the spiritual being that you are in this lifetime. They are just a thought away and often send you signs that they are near.

Their detailed messages provide undeniable proof that there is indeed an afterlife where they exist in spiritual form.

Your eternal connection with your pet endures physical death, and they continue to guide you and watch over you from the Other Side. They don't want you to grieve any longer than needed and want nothing more than for you to be happy and live your life to the fullest.

Honor Your Gift

To live your best life and honor your talents means taking those first few steps into the unknown. The road may be a little bumpy at first, but the rewards will be worth a few bumps. As I honored my psychic gifts and pursued animal communication, it wasn't always smooth sailing. I endured countless verbal attacks and hateful comments from unenlightened cynics. It would have been much easier to get a regular job and disregard my gifts. Even some family members raised their eyebrow at me and thought I was crazy for continuing my psychic work. In the face of scrutiny and adversity, I stayed true to myself, and it has made all the difference in the world.

As you reflect on the stories in this book, I hope they inspire you to identify your gifts and pursue your God-given talents. Don't let anyone try to change who you are or steer you off your spiritual path. When you stand right in the middle of your truth, opportunities will unfold all around you. When you honor your gift and follow your dreams, you will achieve the deepest level of joy, which benefits all of your pets both here and on the Other Side.

I welcome your comments and feedback, so please send me a note if you feel so inclined.

Thank you for joining me on this incredible journey into the amazing afterlife of animals. I bid you, and all of your beloved pets, peace and abundant blessings.

Affiliations, Films, Books and Psychic Directory

White Light Paranormal Insight Team

www.whitelightparanormalinsight.com

As a member of the White Light Paranormal Team, Karen provides psychic information and pre-impressions as a Remote Psychic Viewer.

~ Guiding Spirits and Empowering People

"Our mission is to assist the living in recognizing and validating what may be paranormal activity and to help find a resolution to the best of our ability. Whenever possible, we also strive to assist those entities that may be in turmoil or unrest."

Documentary Film

All Around Us

www.allaroundusfilm.com

This film features the life of psychic and medium Seth Michael. It will take you behind the scenes to see what it's like to be in Seth's world and a few of his close psychic friends, including Karen Anderson, Animal Communicator.

Books

Hear All Creatures!
The Journey of an Animal Communicator
By Karen Anderson
Available on Amazon and Kindle

Animal lovers everywhere are talking about this book.

Travel down the path with Karen from when she first discovered her talents to the sudden and tragic accident that caused her to shut down her abilities for what she thought was for good, until a little white dove appeared and changed her life forever.

Hear the profound and sometimes tearful messages of hope and healing from the spirit world. Read vivid details of what the Afterlife is like, how it feels, what it looks like, and what our animals are doing over there right now. Find out why we bond with our animals on a level that exceeds even some human relationships.

Learn how you can become closer to your animal companions, and discover what your animals are trying to say to you.

Anyone who has loved an animal, lost an animal, or had to say goodbye to a dear and devoted friend will find the messages in this book insightful and healing.

The Secret Inner Life of Pets
A Leading Psychologist and an Animal Communicator Bring You the
Love and Wisdom of Animals
By Dr. Patricia Carrington, Ph.D.
with Karen Anderson — Animal Communicator
Available on Amazon and Kindle

An unprecedented collaboration between a leading Clinical Psychologist and an Animal Communicator.

Dr. Patricia Carrington, Ph.D., is a teacher, author and pioneer in modern energy psychology techniques for healing. In this book, she offers her unique psychological perspective on the interactions between Animal Communicator Karen Anderson and the animals she works with.

Amazing Paranormal Encounters, Volume 2
By Stellium Books

Karen Anderson contributed the final chapter in this collection of ghostly and paranormal stories.

Contact Karen

Check Karen's website, blog or Facebook for classes, events, or to schedule a session: www.KarenAnderson.net.
Online Animal Communication Courses
https://animal-communication-planet.teachable.com/

Psychic Directory

These are some of my favorite and most gifted psychic friends. I encourage you to discover their talents and be sure to tell them I sent you.

In alphabetical order:

Ankhasha Amenti — Psychic Medium
William Becker — Psychic Medium
Linda Drake — Life Path Healer
Teresa Kleve — Psychic Medium
Sharon Lewis Aurora — Psychic/ Medium / Channel
Barbara Mackey — Psychic Medium
Jason Masuoka — Tarot / Psychic
Seth Michael — Spiritual Advisor / Medium

Pete Orbea — Psychic Medium

Cheri Pang — Psychic Medium

Michael and Marti Parry — Psychic Mediums

Karyn Reece — Psychic Medium

Candia Sanders — Energetic Healer / Psychic

Debbie Smith — Psychic Medium

"The things you are passionate about are not random, they are *your calling*."

~ Fabienne Fredrickson

Made in United States
Orlando, FL
23 March 2024

45099879R00098